The Airman's War 1914-1918

The Airman's War 1914–1918

Matthew Richardson

Pen & Sword
AVIATION

First published in Great Britain in 2025 by
Pen & Sword Aviation
An imprint of
Pen & Sword Books Ltd
Yorkshire - Philadelphia

ISBN 978 1 03610 749 9

A CIP catalogue record for this book is available from the British Library.

Typeset in INDIA by IMPEC eSolutions
Printed and bound in England by CPI (UK) Ltd.

The Publisher's authorised representative in the EU for product safety is Authorised Rep Compliance Ltd., Ground Floor, 71 Lower Baggot Street, Dublin D02 P593, Ireland.
www.arccompliance.com

For a complete list of Pen & Sword titles please contact:

PEN & SWORD BOOKS LIMITED
47 Church Street, Barnsley, South Yorkshire, S70 2AS, England
E-mail: enquiries@pen-and-sword.co.uk
Website: www.pen-and-sword.co.uk

or

PEN AND SWORD BOOKS
1950 Lawrence Rd, Havertown, PA 19083, USA
E-mail: uspen-and-sword@casematepublishers.com
Website: www.penandswordbooks.com

FSC www.fsc.org
MIX
Paper | Supporting responsible forestry
FSC® C013604

Contents

Acknowledgements

It is often said that imitation is the sincerest form of flattery. As a young high school pupil one of my earliest introductions to the history of the First World War came through Peter Liddle's excellent series the *Sailor's War*, the *Soldier's War* and the *Airman's War*. Later as a student at the University of Leeds I was fortunate enough to meet Peter, and later still to work alongside him. So, I hope sincerely that he will not mind that in taking inspiration for this volume from Peter's own work, and in homage to it, I have borrowed his title. Where the two books fundamentally differ, however, is that I believed it would be an instructive development not just to explore the British airman's war, as Peter had so masterfully done, but to weave in amongst the British stories some personal testimony from the other side of the line, from little known German accounts.

Like Peter before me I have drawn heavily on my own archival sources. Many of the illustrations herein are the product of long hours spent at postcard fairs in pre-internet days, when some historic images could be found for £1 or £2. Others, however, came from generous friends and contacts. I think particularly of Jo Edkins in this context, also Stuart Brown. Likewise, my late friend Patrick Gariepy provided one of the images from his collection. John and Emily Ford provided assistance with research, which proved to be most useful.

Matthew Richardson,
Douglas, Isle of Man,
2025

Introduction

To later generations, the war in the air between 1914 and 1918 was not tainted with the sense of futility that accompanied that on the ground. In the 1930s, youngsters read of the heroics of Biggles. In the 1970s the 'Airfix generation' grew up with models of Fokker Triplanes and Sopwith Camels, absorbing these stories of dashing pilots. This focus on the elite few, however, belies the fact that the story of the Royal Flying Corps (RFC), Royal Naval Air Service (RNAS) and Royal Air Force (RAF) was far more complex than many have appreciated. There was a highly technical side to the aviation service, and its success was as much about the air mechanics, the riggers and fitters who kept the machines going, as it was about the pilots who got all the glory. Moreover, the mainstream published literature has tended to focus wholly on the fighter aces of RFC in France, to the detriment of the work of the RNAS in other theatres and at sea, and of airship or bomber crews. More than this, in 1914 there was no precedent for a war fought in the air. These men were pioneers, who developed the doctrines and tactics of aerial combat from scratch, as they went along.

This book is not intended to document every model and type of aircraft in use during the First World War. Aficionados and students of the air war will also recognise that it is not possible to give an in-depth account of every aspect of the history of the air services in a volume of this size. It would take a series of such books; indeed, the highly detailed journal *Cross and Cockade* has been running for some forty years, and as yet shows no sign of a shortage of material.

Instead, this book seeks to give a flavour of various aspects of service in the air arms, to demonstrate how diverse were the myriads of different experiences of their personnel across the globe between 1914 and 1918. It uses wherever possible the words of those who were actually there, to convey a sense of immediacy. It also follows the ethos of Peter Liddle's original book in that every person who is featured was, at the time of the events, of the rank of squadron commander or below.

Chapter One

1914

Like Topsy the RNAS was not born on a certain day; it just grew. The beginning of the RNAS is inseparable from the beginning of aviation itself. Within six years of the first demonstration of the practical possibilities of the heavier than-air machine by the Wright brothers, the Admiralty had established an aeronautical branch. That was in 1909. Though its resources were temporary absorbed into the RFC, as the Naval Wing, by July 1914 it had re-emerged as an independent formation.

By contrast Britain's RFC had existed for only twenty-eight months when it had to go to war in August 1914. It had undertaken a practice mobilisation in spring 1914, but at no time during this concentration of the whole strength of the RFC was it possible to put more than thirty machines into the air at once, giving some idea of the strength of the corps at the time. Perhaps because of its small size, it was one of the most efficient and highly disciplined formations in the British Army. This was in part due to the fact that many of its early NCOs were transfers from the Grenadier Guards, the adjutant, Lieutenant Barrington-Kennett, being a guardsman himself. The Royal Engineers had also contributed largely to the personnel, and in its pre-war years at least the RFC tried to live up to Barrington-Kennett's vow that the corps should combine the smartness of the Grenadier Guards with the efficiency of the sappers.

When on 4 August 1914 Britain declared war on Germany, the Military Wing of the RFC comprised 147 officers, 1,097 men and 179 aeroplanes. There were seven aeroplane squadrons: No. 1 Squadron at Brooklands was in the process of converting from being 'The Airship Detachment RFC'; No. 2 Squadron was moving from Montrose in Scotland to Netheravon; No. 3 Squadron was at Netheravon; 'A' and 'B' Flights of No. 4 Squadron were at Eastchurch and 'C' Flight was at Netheravon; No. 5 Squadron was at Gosport; No. 6 Squadron was at South Farnborough; and No. 7 Squadron was at Farnborough, where it was disbanded on 8 August 1914 to provide additional staff to the other squadrons. Famous British ace James McCudden was a lowly air mechanic with the RFC at this time, and remembered,

> No. 3 Squadron embarked on the evening of August 12th, 1914, at about 6 p.m., on a very small tramp steamer called the *Dee*. Many jokes have been passed since about the good ship *Dee*. The voyage proved uneventful, and we sighted the French coast about 1 p.m., and I know there were many silent thoughts of what lay in store for us over there. However, it was generally expected that we should all be home by Christmas. We disembarked at 3 p.m., and then proceeded to unload our transport. There were many French people about, who all seemed very pleased to see us, all shouting out something which I could not understand, but it sounded to me like 'Live

long and tear'. Subsequent acquaintance with the French language leads me to believe that they said '*Vive l' Angleterre*'.

We spent the night of the 13th sleeping on the pave on the quay, and at about 4 a.m. had breakfast, biscuits and bacon, after which I boarded a Daimler touring tender, driven by a man named Chapman, and together with Lieutenant Cruickshank and three other fellows set off for Amiens, by way of Montreuil and Abbeville.

We found our own Squadron, and my first thought was my machine. I found Lieutenant Conran sitting under the 'Parasol', with his shirt sleeves rolled up as it was awfully hot. I reported with the rigger, one Abrahams, who had been with me over a year on Lieutenant Conran's machine, and forthwith we started to fit little wooden racks to carry small hand grenades, which were to be used as bombs, because at the commencement of hostilities we had nothing in the way of aerial bombs of any sort whatever. These hand grenades were extremely local in effect, and I don't suppose they ever did much damage except when dropped in among troops. We also received some fléchettes, or steel darts, for dropping, but it was very obvious that these would not do much harm unless dropped on troops with no head cover. We dropped a lot of these, but I never heard whether they did much harm.[1]

Among the pilots of No. 5 Squadron was Lieutenant Gordon Bayly who on 12 August 1914 flew his machine from Dover to Amiens in France, and then onwards to Maubeuge, which 8 years before, British and French military staff had agreed would be the assembly point for an expeditionary force of 100,000 British troops should there be an invasion of neutral Belgium. The RFC quickly mobilised some 860 officers and men at Maubeuge, with all 20 of its remaining aeroplanes (2 had crashed en route). McCudden describes his arrival after a weary journey on the road. Just as with horses in the cavalry, tending to the aeroplanes was the first priority:

> We arrived in Maubeuge about 9 [pm] at night very tired and dusty. I found my machine and forthwith renewed an exhaust valve in the engine as it had distorted. The machines had mostly arrived about 4 p.m., and when I saw Mr. Conran he said that the exhaust valve went with a devil of a bang, and he thought one of his grenades had exploded in his machine. However, much to his relief, nothing happened and so he landed at Maubeuge all right. We erected our flight hangar, and put two machines in it, with a squeeze, and then we settled down for the night. At Maubeuge we were given a large French blanket each, and so my rigger and I combined forces and used one blanket for a mattress, and the other as a quilt.[2]

As British land forces assembled in France, civilians reported German troops in large numbers advancing through Brussels south-west towards Mons, 30 miles away. The RFC was now to perform the role for which it had been conceived, by confirming or disproving the rumours through aerial observation. At 10.16 am on 22 August 1914, Bayly took off in Avro 504A No. 390, flying as observer with pilot Second Lieutenant Vincent Waterfall – the rule that two pilots must not fly together had already been overridden by the urgent need for qualified observers. Waterfall was born in Grimsby in 1891, and was commissioned into the 3rd Battalion, East Yorkshire Regiment in 1912. He trained as a pilot at the Vickers School in 1913 and gained RAeC Certificate No. 461 on 22 April 1914. In many ways, his progress was similar to that of Bayly, as his flying career had evolved from simple straight flights and circuits to more complex manoeuvres. By April 1914 he was familiar with the new Martinsyde monoplane and went on to become Martinsyde Company's pilot.

Now he found himself flying at 2,000ft, piloting Avro 504A No. 390 over the Enghien-Soignies area. At around 10.50 am, they made a pass at just a couple of hundred feet over some enemy troops. The Germans were at first so surprised that they failed to fire a single shot at an easy target, flying low and slow. The aeroplane next banked and made the mistake of returning towards one of the columns; their reception was considerably more hostile this time, and the Avro crashed by the roadside. At a time when anti-aircraft fire was more luck than science, and German conscripts were not known for their marksmanship, the untrained riflemen must have been stunned by their own shooting in bringing down the first British aeroplane to be lost. These men, from the 12th Brandenburg Grenadier Regiment, claimed the kill. Their captain, the writer Walter Bloem, wrote,

> Suddenly a plane flew over us ... I told off two groups to fire at it, and soon everyone seemed to be firing at it. It turned back as if to return southward but too late: its nose turned down, it made several corkscrew turns, and then fell like a stone about a mile or so away. Murmurs of satisfaction all round. A little later three Hussars came past and shouted that they had found the plane in a field further on. 'What about the pilot and observer?' I asked. 'Both in bits, sir'.[3]

Bayly and Waterfall were not carrying parachutes, but at their low altitude they would have been useless anyway. They died on impact, and little of the wreckage was left after burning fuel incinerated the doped canvas and ash frame. Uncertain what to do with their first dead foe – the fallen fliers they called 'Black Angels' – the soldiers removed their caps, fired a volley of musketry over the smoking wreckage and covered them with a few inches of soil. Nearby Belgians placed flowers for those who had flown to rescue them from invasion. Later, the local landowner exhumed the corpses and placed them in zinc coffins, hidden in his distillery cellar to await a proper burial. For the German commander, von Kluck, the wrecked Avro and bodies in RFC flying tunics provided the first proof that the British Expeditionary Force (BEF) was on the continent of Europe.

For airmen, the threat that was certainly present on the ground would soon also become a reality in the air. The defence of the aeroplane was the duty of the observer, but at best, at this time he would have carried a carbine, shotgun or revolver;

the first Lewis gun would not be mounted on an Avro until October 1914. In these early days, the very act of flying was regarded as so precarious that that even attempting to interfere with an enemy as they carried out their own reconnaissance was not actively considered. Opposing aircraft sometimes passed each other if not exactly with a wave, then at a safe distance. Only later was it considered wise to try to prevent an enemy making it back to base with his report. Lieutenant William Read was with No. 3 Squadron, and his testimony confirms that not only was his machine unarmed, but offensive action against an enemy was also not even contemplated. In his diary, he records how unusual his observer's warlike attitude was at the time,

> One day, after our reconnaissance over Mons and Charleroi, Jackson spotted a German Taube machine. I had also seen him but we had done our job and I did not want a fight. Jackson was always bloodthirsty, however, and the following shouted conversation ensued:
> Jackson: 'Look, old boy!'
> Me: 'Yes, I know.'
> Jackson: 'I think we ought to go for him, old boy.'
> Me: 'Better get home with your report.'
> Jackson: 'I think we ought to go for him, old boy.'
> Me: 'All right.'
> I changed course for him and, as we passed the Taube, Jackson got in two shots with the rifle. We turned and passed each other again with no obvious result. This happened three or four times. Then, 'Have you got a

> revolver, old boy? My ammunition's all gone.' I, feeling rather sick of the proceedings, said 'Yes. But no ammo.' 'Give it to me, old boy, and this time fly past him as close as you can.' I carried out instructions and, to my amazement, as soon as we got opposite the Taube, Jackson, with my Army issue revolver grasped by the barrel, threw it at the Taube's propeller. Of course it missed and then, honour satisfied, we turned for home.[4]

After battling overwhelming German forces at Mons, the BEF had no option but to retire, and began its long retreat towards Paris. One RFC ground crewman, sadly now anonymous, recalled the constant harassment from German aircraft,

> … my unit, the 4th Squadron, Royal Flying Corps, together with the 2nd, 3rd and 5th Squadrons, went with the British Expeditionary Force to France on August 11, 1914. We moved in separate units by motor convoy, from Boulogne to a place north of Maubeuge, travelling via Abbeville and St. Quentin. I shall never forget the warm reception we received from the civilian population. And, at a very little village, the chorus of children continually chanting *Viva l'Angleterre* as we passed by. Our planes, which actually flew from England, consisted of B.E. biplanes and Bleriot mono-planes [*sic*], and the only weapons the pilots carried was a revolver, the same as the rank and file. A few days before the Battle of Mons we had our first casualty, a N.C.O. acting as observer, being wounded whilst doing a reconnaissance. Unlike

the French and Belgian planes we had no identification marks, and our planes in consequence were often attacked by friend and foe. As a result it was decided to mark the underside of the bottom plane with a large Union Jack, and that appeared to solve the problem. On August 24 the battle of Mons was at its height, and during that afternoon we had to move as quickly as possible to escape being overrun.

The long retreat afterwards provided many exciting incidents for our troops, but I do not think anything could have equalled the endurance and skill of our pilots (all officers of crack Army regiments at that time), for despite the difficulty of having to make landings on improvised landing grounds, not one plane was even damaged. During the retreat the German planes located us each day, and on one particular day, September 1, we were rather shocked when a German plane boldly circled over us and then dropped four bombs. This, I imagine, was the first ever aerial bomb raid and, as there were no anti-aircraft guns at that time, you can imagine the resentment that raid caused among us. The raiding Hun was chased by our only fighter plane, a Martinsyde Scout, capable of a record speed of 90 miles an hour, but without result. The retreat brought us as far as Melun, and when our cavalry turned the enemy back nearby, we advanced as far as Le Fare-en Tardenwaire [Tardenois] and then the whole R.F.C. got to work with that vigour and zeal which was carried on for the duration of the war. Looking back 40 years, August 1914 was a great test

> of endurance for our troops, but still one feels proud to have taken part in that memorable page of history of the Royal Flying Corps.[5]

In fact, numerous British diaries note the presence of a German 'Taube' overhead during the Retreat but dismiss it as ineffective because it did not drop any bombs, little realising its role in reconnaissance. The pilot of one such German aircraft, flying over the Forêt de Mormal, was Unteroffizier Werner, who wrote of his patrol,

> I had received the order to ascertain the positions of the English and French troops after the English defeat at Mons. An officer went along as an observer. We flew first in a southern direction along the main road to Paris, leading us past a splendid wood, in which about 40,000 inhabitants from this area have sought shelter. After around a one-hour flight by which we could ascertain the fact that the Englishmen had withdrawn – we saw possibly a hundred abandoned vehicles still there, and not too far from this place, the French artillery together with the English infantry had taken up a new position – the observation officer did a sketch and we turned back.
>
> At this moment I saw about 300 meters above me a Bristol twin-decker, which pursued us. We were possibly at a height of 1,600 meters. As my monoplane had a lower speed than the Bristol, he soon caught up with us. In vain I attempted to get away from the enemy; however, I did not succeed. On the contrary, the Bristol always

kept with us. My God, when would the bomb, which we expected any minute, hit us! The twin-decker descended further and further and was barely 150 meters above us.

We had the same feeling that a bird must have, if a falcon is floating above him. We believed that the enemy approached nearer to have a better target for his bomb. We pulled our revolvers out and started to shoot. It had become clear to us, in the meantime, that fortunately the Englishman had no bombs or that he could not fire them in front of his aeroplane, because the engine and propeller were right at the front.

It was a dreadfully exciting moment. The twin-decker had sunk even further and now the battle began on both sides. The observer and pilot of the double-decker opened fire, when we at the same height and about 150 meters apart. Obviously they only had guns and did not dare to get closer, because they were afraid that we could throw our own bombs. Minute on minute went by. It seemed like hours to us. I had the feeling that my machine had reached its limit, and believed any minute that my end had come. This lasted half an hour. Then my observer patted me on the shoulder and pointed out to me, about 300 meters higher, a small French Bleriot, in a frantic haste in our direction to help the Bristol twin-decker.

He travelled in circles around round us and the bullets whistled around our ears. But suddenly above the rattle of the engine we heard the explosions of artillery. We were above the German lines, and our side were firing on the Bristol and Bleriot.[6]

At this stage in the war, the ground crews (except for those few air mechanics who flew with pilots in case of mechanical breakdown) were suffering the same hardships as the infantry, as the Retreat from Mons went on day after weary day. The squadron support parties, which moved by road, were caught up in the chaos and confusion of the Retreat. With rations unreliable, they lived off the land. McCudden was lucky in this regard, recalling 'At about 6 a.m. on August 26th we had breakfast with "C" Flight Officers, who gave us a share of their own food, as we had none.'[7]

Hot weather in August 1914 affected the engines significantly, and often mechanics were cleaning plugs, resetting magnetos, and scraping valves until late at night, sometimes with only their small personal issue of tools to work with. Aeroplanes were left in the open overnight and mechanics slept in the cockpits, under the wings, or if they were lucky in a nearby barn. Often the ground crews received just a few hours' notice to pack up and go, with the very real danger of being cut off. Aircraft could be flown out quickly – if they would start; at Le Cateau, a Henri Farman was burned because its engine refused to cooperate and would not be left for the enemy. Packing up aeroplane tenders and workshop lorries took longer. At Juilly, previous army training came in handy when a party of air mechanics were told off to line a sunken road armed with rifles, to enable No. 3 Squadron to get away.

Steadily, however, air power was beginning to show what it was capable of, and numerous times airmen demonstrated the potential of this new weapon. In terms of reconnaissance information, it was invaluable, even if the lack of clear national markings on aeroplanes caused some difficulties. Lieutenant Louis Strange flew with No. 5 Squadron, in Henri Farman No. 341, and remembered,

> On September 11 … I made six flights with Lieut. Rabagliati as my passenger, after which I landed to report to the Corps headquarters. Unfortunately this had been shifted from the locality where I had received overnight instructions to make my report. Before I realised what the trouble was, we found ourselves surrounded at a respectable distance by a regiment of Zouaves. The next five minutes might have been amusing to an onlooker, but I cannot say I found them so. I was not at all sure of the nationality of these troops, and evidently they had decided to take no risks about mine. Half a dozen rifle bullets whizzed round our ears. Then a little old French officer on a white pony galloped up to our field and stopped the shooting. I had not put my engine off, but kept it going with the switches, and every time I switched on to keep it running, rifles all round the field went up to the 'present'. The French officer remained about two hundred yards away from us, where he did his best to keep his restive pony quiet; whenever the animal gave him a moment's leisure, he waved a white handkerchief frantically up and down.
>
> Whether this was a token of surrender or an incitement to us to give ourselves up quietly or merely the anticipation of a fond farewell, I could not gather, but we thought it

> best to humour him by returning the compliment. I had, however, decided that I could not afford to waste the time involved in giving him a satisfactory explanation of our identity; I therefore opened up the engine and headed the machine in the direction of the ancient sportsman, thinking that if the soldiers started to shoot at me again while I was taking off, the nearer to their officer I was the fewer risks I should run.
>
> The pony took fright at what it very naturally thought to be an uncouth monster. It bolted, and the officer fell off. The foremost Zouaves rushed forward to pick up and save their officer; those behind them thought discretion the better part of valour and rushed away to save themselves. Consequently my Henri Farman took off between the flustered old gentleman on the ground and his bolting pony; amid much excitement and a few odd rifle shots, we waved a last farewell and dived behind a convenient wood...[8]

It was a reconnaissance flight by the RFC that had established that the German columns had now begun to retreat away from Paris, and a few days after that, a daring raid by Lieutenant Gilbert Mapplebeck of No. 4 Squadron demonstrated what else might be possible with aircraft. Whilst on reconnaissance, he came across a German transport column of thirteen wagons. He had three bombs with him, and these he used to such effect that within minutes the entire column was a smoking ruin. The wagons were laden with explosives. The first bomb landed near the tail end. In Mapplebeck's own words 'That began the firework display.'[9] The other bombs he dropped near the centre, and these triggered a series of terrific explosions, which enveloped the column. Not surprisingly, he was awarded a Distinguished Service Order (DSO). McCudden remembered early efforts at bombing by No. 3 Squadron,

> We were now receiving fairly large size bombs for disposal. One type, which was painted red, weighed ten pounds, and had a small parachute attached to give it directional stability; it was called a shrapnel bomb. Another new type, which was called the Mélinite bomb, weighed twenty-six pounds, and had a striker in the nose to detonate it. This bomb was really a converted French shell, and was afterwards condemned as being highly unsafe. I mention these types of bombs because they were our early attempts at producing this very necessary adjunct to aerial warfare.
>
> Mr. Conran one morning left the aerodrome on the Blériot Parasol to bomb Laon railway station, with the following loads of bombs: Sixteen hand grenades, two shrapnel bombs, each one in a rack on the outside of the fuselage, out of which the pilot had to throw them by hand, and a Mélinite bomb tied on to an upper fuselage longeron with string, so that when he wanted to unload this bomb he had to cut the string first with a knife and then push the bomb overboard. This outfit will perhaps enlighten the present-day bomb droppers as to the disadvantages we experienced in our early efforts at strafing the Boche from the air.[10]

By the outbreak of the First World War in August 1914, the RNAS had more aircraft under its control than the RFC. The navy maintained twelve airship stations around the coast of Britain from Longside, Aberdeenshire in the north-east to Anglesey in the west. One of the pioneers of naval aviation in airships was Lieutenant John Fletcher – actually an army officer, who had been one of the first volunteers for the Air Battalion of the Royal Engineers. Fletcher had qualified in balloon flying just before the outbreak of war, recalling that,

> At the end of my training I had to pass two tests a solo flight at night and a solo flight by day. The night flight was quite uneventful but the day flight was extremely interesting. A very light wind carried me to Amersham and it was there I decided to land. I saw a field of about an acre on my side of the town and so I pulled the plug to let the gas out, but instead of going down I went up! I got to about 6,000 feet and then suddenly the balloon started to come down again. I landed in the field I had originally picked out and I got out of the basket to see what had happened. To my surprise I saw the balloon had collapsed. The answer it turned out was that after it had collapsed the updraft of a cumulus cloud I had not seen because of the canopy had carried the balloon up. Then it escaped and came down again. In other words I had parachuted down.[11]

He was subsequently posted to the RNAS station at Kingsnorth, near Chatham. Here he was in command of HM

Airship No. 4, with an all-Royal Navy (RN) crew, when it carried out the first air patrol of the war, between Southend and Margate, on 5 August 1914. It was not an auspicious start to hostilities, as Fletcher remembered,

> Off Margate some Territorial soldiers decided the airship was a Zeppelin and started firing on it, and that despite the fact that we had a White Ensign flying the size of a room![12]

A week later the airship was covering the embarkation of the BEF to France when a propeller blade came off somewhere between Dover and Calais, and had to be repaired whilst airborne.

One of the stalwarts of the RNAS in 1914 was Major E.L. Gerrard, Royal Marine Light Infantry (RMLI), who commanded the squadron that made the first attack on Germany from the sky, on 22 September 1914, when the RNAS launched an air attack from Antwerp on the Zeppelin sheds at Düsseldorf and Cologne. In this attack he was flying in B.E.2a, serial No. 50 (undoubtedly the most famous bomber of 1914, No. 50 was nominally the personal aircraft of Commander Charles Rumney Samson). No. 50 was followed by No. 149, a Sopwith Churchill, No. 169 a Sopwith Tabloid and No. 906, an impressed Sopwith Tractor Biplane. At this early stage of the air war, none of these aircraft bore any marking other than their black serial number on a white patch.

One of the other pilots who took part in this action was Lieutenant C.H. Collet, Royal Marine Artillery (RMA), who was also serving in the Eastchurch Wing under Samson, by then operating on the exposed left flank of the Allied armies near Dunkirk. Because of thick mist on 22 September, only Collet reached his target, dropping two 20lb bombs from 400ft on to the Zeppelin sheds at Düsseldorf. This was the first successful bombing raid ever carried out, and for his exploit Collet was awarded the DSO. The citation read,

> On 22 September 1914, flying a Sopwith Tractor Biplane [he] made a successful attack on the German Zeppelin Airship shed at Dusseldorf. Lieut. Collet's feat is notable – gliding down from 6,000 feet, the last 1500 in mist, he finally came in sight of the Airship shed at a height of 400 feet, only a quarter of a mile away from it.[13]

Unlike the RFC, at the beginning of the war the RNAS possessed two aeroplanes armed with guns and both were based at Eastchurch. One mounted a Lewis gun, the other a Maxim, and in addition one airship carried a Hotchkiss; ten months later the Admiralty would still be complaining bitterly that the allocation of Lewis guns to the RNAS was totally inadequate. When the RNAS went to war, their principal airborne weapons were handguns. The most widely available of these was the army's Short Lee-Enfield rifle in the standard .303-in calibre; known as the SMLE.

In 1920 (as a group captain) Gerrard compiled some notes for the Air Historical Branch of the Air Ministry. His comments cover the early days at Eastchurch, from November

1914 onwards. Some are of particular interest in relation to early armament,

> Aerial gunnery was obviously about to become of greater importance. The first machine we had in which the armament formed part of the design was the Vickers gunbus. It was a steel 'pusher' with only a 100hp Gnome engine. It was unpopular among pilots for various reasons. It was heavy and gave insufficient climb when fully loaded with full tanks, a maxim and a crew of two. It was also sluggish and heavy on the controls, especially the rudder. It was eventually crashed by Warrant Officer Alcock [later to be first to fly the Atlantic Ocean with Lieutenant Brown in a twin-engined Vickers Vimy bomber]. The earliest armament was probably the twelve bore gun carried in the Blériot Parasol. It was mounted upon the starboard plane and inclined to the aft of the machine so as to clear the propeller tips. Chain shot ammunition was used, small lead balls connected by a short length of steel cable. Both hands were required to reload both barrels – a difficult operation in a non-stable machine. The range was short and accurate shooting very difficult to obtain. We never obtained any results with it in service.[14]

The Isle of Man Steam Packet Company, having one of the most modern fleets in British home waters, made an important contribution to the war at sea. Of the fifteen steamers owned by the company in 1914, eleven were either chartered or requisitioned by the British government for war service. *Ben-my-Chree* and *Viking* both served as seaplane carriers and were converted by the addition of a rear hangar. *Viking* was renamed HMS *Vindex* for the duration of the war, as there was already an HMS *Viking* in the Royal Navy. Similarly, the Chatham and Southeastern Railway steamer *Engadine* was requisitioned from cross-Channel duties and became a floatplane carrier.

HMS *Engadine* participated in another notable early RNAS action, the December 1914 Cuxhaven Raid. From the outbreak of war on 4 August 1914, Captain Cecil Francis Kilner, RMLI was flying seaplanes on patrol in the North Sea from Royal Naval Air Stations Clacton and Westgate and with the detached RNAS unit at Ostend, but this force withdrew when the Belgian garrison retired to Dunkirk. His DSO citation records that,

> On the 25th December 1914, an air reconnaissance of the Heligoland Bight, including Cuxhaven, Heligoland and Wilhelmshaven was made by seven naval seaplanes, and the opportunity was taken at the same time of attacking with bombs, points of military importance. The reconnaissance involved combined operations with light cruisers and destroyers, and submarines watching inshore and ready to render aid if necessary.
>
> The vessels detailed having arrived at the rendezvous before daylight, as soon the light was sufficient, the seaplanes were hoisted out (from HMS *Engadine*) and dispatched. At the beginning of the flight the weather was clear, but on nearing land the seaplanes met with thick

> weather and were compelled to fly low, thus becoming exposed to a heavy fire at a short range. Several machines were hit, but all remained in the air for three hours and succeeded in obtaining valuable information regarding dispositions of the enemy's ships and defences. Bombs were dropped on military points.
>
> Capt. Kilner's and two other machines regained their ship. Three others, short of fuel, were compelled to descend and their pilots were saved by Submarine 'E1' although subjected to fire from an airship. The pilot of the remaining sea plane, having lost his bearings, was compelled to descend after 3 ½ hours flight, owing to engine trouble and was rescued by a Dutch trawler and returned safely to England.[15]

This last machine was piloted by Flight Commander F.E.T. Hewlett, who recalled,

> I was the first to start, leaving one of the vessels in the flotilla at about seven o'clock [am] on Christmas morning. The weather conditions then, from the point of view of aviation, were all that could be desired. It was quite calm, and there was no sign of fog. I was flying in a Short Seaplane and, when I started off, went to a height of about 2,000 feet. I made direct for the coast near Cuxhaven, but when I got near the shore the fog came over awfully thick, and I was obliged to descend to about 200 feet. It was generally impossible to see anything, but there were occasional glimpses of

clearness. The first thrilling incident that occurred was when I sighted some German war vessels. I could not say precisely what type of vessel they were, but they sighted me, and immediately opened fire. I think they used the usual 'pom-pom' description of shell. They used plenty of shells, but I was lucky, for neither the machine, nor myself was hit, and I managed to get quite clear. The fog was very thick, and for obvious reasons I did not attempt to drop any bombs. After passing out of sight of the enemy's ships, I flew direct for the shore near Cuxhaven. The fog was frightfully thick, and although flying very low I was only able to catch fleeting glimpses of the coastline. The fog showed no indication of lifting, and as it was obviously useless to go on flying, I decided to return. I was at this time actually over the land near Cuxhaven. I could see the ground very faintly when the mist now and then lifted for a few minutes.

On the return, after flying a little while I found myself over clear water, and so endeavoured to get back to the British vessels. This was at about nine o'clock [am], after I had been in the air for two hours. Suddenly a hostile aircraft came out of the clouds. It was about 600 feet away from me and some 500 feet above me. The enemy aviators immediately opened fire, but here again good fortune favoured me, and I got my machine and myself clear away. At about half-past nine [am] my machine began to give some trouble. The fault was not due to an insufficiency of oil, but to a small failure in the oiling system. But although so slight, I knew at once

> that I would be compelled very soon to descend, and so I looked round for some vessel near which I could alight. Here again I was very lucky. I sighted a vessel which I thought to be a Dutch trawler. I descended to a distance which enabled me to see her clearly, and finding that I was correct in my first assumption of her nationality, I alighted alongside.[16]

Another of the officers taking part in the raid on Cuxhaven was Flight Sub-Lieutenant Vivian Gaskell Blackburn, RN, who was born and brought up in Leeds. He was the youngest son of Mr H. Gaskell Blackburn, who resided at Bank House, Horsforth in the north of the city. Mr Blackburn was naturally delighted to hear of his son's role in the mission, and remarked to a journalist

'One cannot help being proud of the feat, and the fact that my son was the youngest pilot of the lot.'[17]

His father added that Blackburn was only 22 years of age, and was at first articled to a land agent, but he gave this up to go forward with aviation, in which he was keenly interested. He began to receive instruction in flying at the Bristol Flying School, Brooklands, and in September 1913 qualified as an airman. He was appointed to a temporary commission in the RNAS after the outbreak of the war, although he had applied for a commission before the conflict started, under the scheme devised by Winston Churchill, whereby qualified pilots were granted posts in the Royal Navy. Perhaps the most famous Cuxhaven participant of all was Lieutenant Robert Erskine Childers, author of the novel *Riddle of the Sands* (1903), who flew on the mission as an observer with Kilner. The novel was set in the Friesian Islands and Childers's familiarity with the north German coastline around Cuxhaven meant that he played a key part in planning the raid. During the action he made an accurate reconnaissance of the German ships in the Schillig Roads.

Despite the somewhat limited results of the raid, the action had seen several pioneering activities. Surface, sub-surface and aerial forces had cooperated in a combined form of operation never previously undertaken. Launching and recovering aircraft on the open sea during an operational situation had not been attempted before, but went well, though favourable conditions helped. The rescue role of the submarines, planned but not tested, had proved vital and was to be used again. The Admiralty felt that they had scored a moral victory, their small force sailing close to the German coast undisturbed by the High Seas Fleet, which had remained in harbour. Above all, in later years the Royal Navy was deeply proud of the fact that there was no Christmas truce in the war at sea.

Chapter Two

Home Operations and Training

When the RFC departed for France in 1914 the air defence of the United Kingdom was left, initially at least, largely in the hands of the RNAS. Those RFC units that did remain behind were mainly training establishments. In previous wars civilians had in the most part remained safe and unscathed in their homes; this war now brought with it a terrifying new dimension – attack from the air – and methods and equipment would have to be developed, from scratch, to deal with it effectively. Initially, however, the main threat to Britain's survival came from U-boats.

RNAS seaplane aircraft offered the most rapid possible response to enemy submarine sightings, although it remained tactically difficult to attack an alert U-boat before it could submerge. Wing Commander John Cyril Porte, RNAS Felixstowe, was one of the navy's pioneering submariners, who later joined the air branch. He had worked for American Glenn Curtiss before 1914 and was familiar with seaplane technology. Improved flying boats of the 'America' model, known as H-4 ('Small America') and H-8 ('Large America') were imported from the United States for use by the RNAS. However, the H-8s were found to be underpowered, and so were equipped with 250-hp Rolls-Royce engines instead, the improved flying boats now being designated as H-12. These machines offered a powerful anti-submarine patrol capability that had previously been lacking. The multi-engine flying boats were suitable for searching large areas of ocean over many hours and, although long patrols could be exhausting for the crews, the flying boats possessed both the speed and payload required to carry out attacks against submarines caught in the open. Porte continued to engineer improvements, and new RNAS variants began to enter service late in 1917. The F.2A model, powered by two 345-hp Rolls-Royce engines and equipped with half a dozen Lewis guns and up to 500lb of bombs, could patrol for up to six hours. The final version was the Felixstowe F.5L, which entered service in 1918.

Royal Naval Air Stations around Britain's coast allowed fighter and bomber squadrons to protect shipping from hostile forces. Flight Sub-Lieutenant Austin Bradford Hill trained first at Chrystal Palace in 1916, before attending the training school at Chingford. He remembered,

> For the first two weeks a recruit did no flying. He absorbed the atmosphere (mainly of engine oil) and performed chores. The one which stays in my mind was the manhandling of aircraft into the hangers at the end of the day. A member of my group was Ivor Novello, later of musical comedy fame. To the tune that first brought him fame, 'Keep the Home Fires Burning', we sang:
>
> Keep poor B class stowing
> Though the lorry's going
> Though the lorry's due to leave

The aerodrome.
There's another Maurice
Waiting out there for us,
We must shove the damned thing in
Or we can't go home.

Ivor was a great writer of tunes and an asset to the officers' mess. For his own, and others', safety his flying career was brief. At this time, too, one of the instructors was Ben Travers, the author of *Rookery Nook* and the many Aldwych farces. He once took a Maurice-Farman biplane and a shotgun in pursuit of a Zeppelin.

I completed my training with some dummy bomb dropping and a few cross country jaunts (not too far, for we had no maps and no compass). Finally I looped the loop to mark my freedom and the fact that I was ready for 'active service'. The Fates were kind, for in the spring of 1917 I was posted to East Fortune, a vast aerodrome south of Edinburgh and the home of airships (later the R34). The main task of the two aircraft pilots was to escort battleships down the Firth of Forth and, armed with bombs, to seek German submarines, which occasionally torpedoed merchant ships off the coast of St Abb's head some 20 miles away. I never saw one. Otherwise I was free to put in many hours of peaceful flying and thus to graduate to the more advanced types of aircraft – the Bristol Bullet and the Sopwith Pup. One of the former turned upside down when a tyre burst at landing. I was left hanging head downwards, helpless but unharmed.

> On another occasion I took it up to 15,000 feet, which without oxygen must have been a little unsafe. Anyway, the engine did not like it and packed up. I had a long glide down with the propeller hanging dead but no serious problem with the vast grassy expanse of aerodrome on which to land (we had no runways in those days).[1]

From this station Hill frequently visited Sir Edward Sharpey Schafer, the distinguished professor of physiology at the University of Edinburgh, who lived by the sea in North Berwick. In his garden they would play a game of bowls together and Lady Schafer provided a gorgeous tea. This wartime idyll, including twenty minutes aloft in a coastal airship, came to an end in June 1917, when Hill was posted to the Aegean.

Further stations were constructed and the Royal Navy's fleet of airships was greatly expanded. The Submarine Scout (SS) series that were developed during the war would go on to prove invaluable in patrolling busy sea lanes around the coast. The Submarine Scout and later Submarine Scout Zero (SSZ) class were particularly valuable on convoy escort duty. These aircraft as well as carrying light armament themselves, had the capacity to use wireless to call up naval vessels for depth charge attacks. The experiences of airship crews are perhaps the least known but are not without drama. For example, while on patrol over the Bristol Channel on the morning of 18 January 1917 the engine of SS.15 started giving problems. The captain, Sub-Lieutenant Cyril J. Pyke then ordered his W/T operator, Frederick Crawford, to climb out on to the narrow landing skid to try to start the engine by swinging the propeller. This was only Crawford's second flight and later he admitted that he had never started an engine before. He was now attempting this task for the first time 1,500ft up in the air, in a 15-kt wind balanced on a narrow strip of wood just 2.5in wide. Pyke then spent the next forty-five minutes trying himself. As he was doing so, the airship was losing altitude. It hit the water hard, and the canopy collapsed on top of the two airmen, struggling in the water. At this point, Pyke discovered that Crawford also could not swim, but both men were rescued by a motor launch.

The Royal Navy was slow to develop reconnaissance aircraft to accompany the Grand Fleet, for two main reasons. Firstly, in terms of detection of its main enemy – the German High Seas Fleet – aircraft were at first deemed to be of limited value. They had short range, and in any case directional wireless techniques already provided information about the movements of the German Fleet. The second reason was that as has already been noted, from September 1914 there was an awareness of the pressing need for the RNAS to fulfil its role in Home Defence. That said, some early experiments in launching aircraft from warships did take place with gun turrets planked over. In these cases, it was necessary later to recover the ditched aircraft by means of a derrick.

The development of the true aircraft carrier, with a flight deck to allow for both landing and take-off, was not long in coming. The work of HMS *Ark Royal* in the Aegean is discussed elsewhere, but HMS *Campania*, a converted Cunard liner, became the first aircraft carrier of any description to work with the Grand Fleet. One of her air mechanics aboard the vessel at Scapa Flow was engine fitter Frederick Mansfield, who remembered that getting airborne from the flight deck was not easy. The ship turned into the wind to launch but even then, seaplanes taking off would dip alarmingly towards the sea and the crew were on standby in case they should hit the water. An axle with rubber tyred wheels was placed under the floats, which would be released as soon as the machine was airborne, and then recovered from the sea. For stowage in the hangars, the seaplanes had folding wings. Mansfield remembered,

> [Deck take-offs] were few and far between. During the 9 months or so that I was aboard *Campania* there were no more than three occasions when this operation took place. To anyone aboard a modern aircraft carrier the whole thing was ludicrous. By the time we had hoisted the seaplane from the hold to the fight deck on the derrick by steam winch, fitted the axle under the floats, spread the wings (this was the Chippy's job) started the engine and got the machine away, most of the morning had gone.[2]

Some of HMS *Campania*'s seaplanes took part in a rather unsuccessful attempt to reconnoitre the islands of Borkum and Juist, whilst in March 1916 the converted ferry HMS *Vindex*, now part of the Harwich Force, took part in a raid on the German airship base at Hoyer. It was not a success, with three of her aircraft forced down by engine failure and falling into enemy hands. Much has been made of the fact that

HMS *Campania* was late leaving Scapa Flow on the morning of the Battle of Jutland. She was then ordered to return to base by Sir John Jellicoe, leaving a significant portion of the fleet without air cover. Only the battlecruisers from Rosyth had such cover, offered by HMS *Engadine*, and one of her Short seaplanes, piloted by Flight Lieutenant F.J. Rutland, provided the only British aerial reconnaissance conducted during the battle. Although he was fired upon, it was a mechanical defect that caused him to land on the water and the aircraft's eventual recall to HMS *Engadine*.

Naval High Command, however, was becoming aware of the possibilities offered by aerial reconnaissance and by the end of the year a new aircraft carrier, HMS *Argus* would be under construction, based upon a half-constructed ocean liner. Another aircraft carrier, HMS *Furious*, had been converted from a ship originally being built as a heavy cruiser. In 1917 a squadron of Sopwith Pups was assigned to her to undertake experimental work on take-off and landing. Take-off into the wind proved to be relatively easy, with the aircraft landing in a nearby field, but the first successful landing on an aircraft carrier occurred on 2 August 1917 when Squadron Commander E.H. Dunning managed to slow his machine on approach to just above stalling speed and it was secured by a deck party. Unfortunately, Dunning was killed a few days later when another attempt went catastrophically wrong. A poignant reminder, the watch he was wearing that day (stopped at 3.45 pm, the time that he died) is on display at the Fleet Air Arm Museum. This tragedy highlighted the fact that at this time HMS *Furious* did not have an adequate flight deck, and it was subsequently lengthened to 300ft. Likewise HMS *Argus* underwent changes to give it a flight deck unobstructed by any funnel or bridgehouse. Flight Lieutenant William F. Dickson remembered,

> HMS *Furious* was one of the three super cruisers. That ship commissioned at Newcastle in June 1917, and we commissioned the ship. From that time onwards I was part of the operational fighter squadron in HMS *Furious*. We also had two seaplanes for reconnaissance but I didn't fly those. We carried out operations, we were at sea almost continuously, on the other side of the North Sea, searching for Zeppelins trying to catch one, and one or two Zeppelins were caught in that way, before they could get out of the range of the fighters. And we had to land in front of the destroyer after completing our mission. The fact was that it was uneconomical to take off and do only one mission before the pilot returned really led to the idea of deck landings, there were six or seven pilots on the ship, landing back on a ship. It all happened in Scapa Flow, because we used to go ashore and practice from an airfield there, we used to practice flying alongside a ship, and run our wheels along the deck to see how possible it was, and that led to official Admiralty trials. Although the landings on the bows of the *Furious* were not successful, well there were two that were successful, but it was obviously regarded by the Admiralty as not being a practical proposition, so they took the ship out of commission and built a landing on

> deck above the funnel structure and mast. The *Furious* continued in commission after that, doing the same operations, I was part of the compliment doing deck flying operation [including] the raid on Tondern carried out from the *Furious* which destroyed two Zeppelins in their hangars.[3]

In August 1917 the Grand Fleet was joined by another seaplane carrier, HMS *Pegasus*. She incorporated several improvements based upon lessons learned from her predecessors. She was constructed with a large box-shaped hangar in her aft section for storage of seaplanes, and a similar hangar built under her bridge to house two small single seater scout aircraft. Aeroplanes could not land directly on her but there was a small moveable flight deck at the bow, which enabled the scout aircraft to take off.

From the very first days of the war, the threat of German Zeppelin airships exercised a disproportionate fear over the British civilian population. Stoked up by a sensationalist press, they, like U-boats were one of the bogey-weapons of the war, developed by ruthless and underhand Huns. As early as September 1914, lighting restrictions were enforced in London. Weeks and months went by however, and apart from the odd sighting off the coast, the Zeppelins did not come. The Germans, despite their reputation for ruthless military efficiency had no immediate offensive plan for the Zeppelins, and too few of them to spare any from reconnaissance duties to bomb Britain. However, pressure was growing for some form of retaliation against the British naval blockade of Germany, and on 19 January 1915 the first Zeppelin raid was launched against Britain. A few bombs were dropped in an ineffectual sortie over Norfolk, but the German crew were building their expertise and as new and more powerful models joined their fleet the raids grew in strength that spring. Newly built hangars in occupied Belgium shortened the range, and in May, London was bombed for the first time. Only at low altitude were the airships in any danger from the aircraft of the RNAS, which were poorly armed and their pilots unused to flying – and landing – at night.

By August 1915, the Imperial German Navy had taken delivery of four new machines of the L.10 class. The growing experience of both German army and navy crews now led to raids with increasing amounts of damage and loss of life. The moonless night of 8 September 1915 prompted the heaviest raid yet. Only one Zeppelin reached its target that night but considerable damage was done, which prompted a public outcry. The official account of the raid recorded that the RNAS had flown only six sorties that night, whilst the RFC had flown none at all. Directly after this incident, Secretary of State for War Lord Kitchener had instructed the RFC to prevent further incursions against the capital. However, there were no trained pilots or efficient aeroplanes that could be spared from the fighting in France, so these would have to come from squadrons in training. Two new landing fields were requisitioned, at Hornchurch and Ilford. Lieutenant Colonel W.G. Salmond, commanding 5th Wing was instructed to make B.E.2c aircraft available at both. Temporary hangars and other necessary equipment were hastily assembled and transported to the airficlds; at least this equipment was held in store – the new pilots presented more of a challenge. Some of the flying officers of No. 23 Squadron that was forming at Gosport had previously been allowed to practice flying at dusk in order to broaden their experience. This was enough to be considered as 'night flying' and seven of them would now form the nucleus of the new air defence of London. One pilot was to be on duty every night at the new airfields, awaiting instruction from the War Office to take off and climb to 8,000ft, with the engine being run and warmed up periodically. Among these officers was Second Lieutenant John Slessor, later to be marshal of the RAF. On his first night at the Hornchurch field he was alerted by a phone call from the War Office to a multi-Zeppelin raid, but fog made taking off impossible. After half an hour it cleared sufficiently to take his B.E. down the runway, lit either side by petrol flares.

His only means of destroying the Zeppelin consisted of four small oblong bombs full of petrol, which the pilot pushed by hand down through a tube in the cockpit floor. In the tube an electrical contact ignited the fuse, whereupon the bomb burst into flames and a bunch of large fish hooks sprang out at the top. These were supposed to catch in the Zeppelin's envelope. When he looked upwards into the dark sky he saw straightaway the huge silver shape, quite silent, of the Zeppelin. It was apparently stationary and was clearly visible in the glow from the lights of London, about 4,000 to 5,000ft above him. He stared, appalled at its vast size. He remembered later that it was like having a cod's eye view of the *Mauretania*. Overcoming his shock and awe he opened the throttle of the B.E. as wide as he dared and began to climb towards the monstrous airship. When Slessor was about 1,000ft below the leviathan, he saw a stream of fiery sparks spill out into the blackness as its engines started up. The huge bulk swung round, cocked its nose up at a sharp angle, and climbed rapidly away from him. Slessor, with his throttle jammed wide open, was on the edge of stalling angle and had no hope at all of catching a Zeppelin climbing with all her engines full out. Finally, he lost her in cloud.

Whilst the army and navy bickered over who should be responsible for the inland defence of the United Kingdom, the Zeppelins struck again in an even more audacious raid in January 1916; nine airships attempted to reach Liverpool, which was completely undefended. Navigational difficulties prevented them reaching their intended target, but bombs were dropped elsewhere. Despite the desperate need for more pilots and aircraft in France, ten new squadrons were allocated for Home Defence, and a new Wing, No. 18, established for defence of London. In April 1916 the first Zeppelin to be brought down by British fire, L15, crashed in the Thames Estuary. She was attacked by Second Lieutenant Alfred Brandon who managed to get above her and dropped a batch of Rankin incendiary darts, but the real cause of her demise was a direct hit from an anti-aircraft gun on the ground. Brandon none the less received a Military Cross (MC) for his efforts. Later that month a fleet of airships attacked London again, but this time they were roughly handled by the capital's much improved air defences. Two of the ships were attacked by aircraft from No. 39 Squadron, piloted by Second Lieutenant William Leefe-Robinson and Captain (later marshal of the RAF) Arthur Harris. During June 1916 the War Office decided that pilots on Home Defence squadrons were being overburdened by the fact that their days were spent in training inexperienced pilots, and their nights spent on Home Defence duties. Henceforth, flying training was removed from the duties of these squadrons. At the same time as the airship raids, the Germans launched a series of 'tip and run' seaplane attacks on south coast towns. Whilst minor in scale, a number of civilians including children, were killed. The response of the RNAS was somewhat haphazard, and on one occasion its aircraft suffered the ignominy of being fired upon by British guns. However, an early home defence success was achieved by Flight Commander R.J. Bone, who forced down a Freidrichshaffen FF33, wounding both crew members.

On 2 September 1916, intelligence decoded from intercepted German signals by the Admiralty's Room 40 indicated that for the first time the German navy and army Zeppelin fleets were combining for the largest raid yet. William Leefe Robinson was on duty that night when the telephone call came. He took off on patrol, and had soon sighted one Zeppelin below him, which he later lost in cloud. When he spotted another some while later, he was determined not to repeat his mistake. He dived at the airship at full speed, positioning himself for an attack from beneath the hull. His first magazine was emptied with little effect, despite the new explosive-incendiary bullets with which he was equipped. A second pass also had no results, but for his final drum of ammunition he aimed for a single point near the tail. This time the airship erupted in flame, and below it Leefe-Robinson fought with his controls to avoid the blazing mass that filled his vision. As the crackling, roaring monster fell past him, he felt the flames scorch his face. The blazing wreck came down at Cuffley, Hertfordshire. None of the crew were saved, indeed most were burned beyond recognition even as a human being. They were buried in the local churchyard, the vicar changing the words of the service from 'our brothers here departed' to 'these men here departed'.

Just over a month later, in the early hours of 1 October 1916, another airship would come down 3 miles to the west of Cuffley in Potters Bar. It was downed by Wulstan Joseph Tempest of No. 39 Home Defence Squadron, who had heard the raiders were en route and ignored orders to patrol the Thames, instead taking his aeroplane to high altitude in an attempt to find them. He was later awarded the DSO. Air Mechanic Clarence W. Thomas writing later in October 1916 to his mother described the event,

> Perhaps by now you, will have heard of the success of one of our pilots. I will try and describe how it happened and all about it. We were warned about ten o'clock [pm] that the Zepps were coming our way, so as usual we turned out to see the fun. Up to 11 o'clock [pm] everything was quiet. Then suddenly the guns started off with a deafening rattle. Our machines immediately went up in the direction of the firing. The searchlight caught her, and we could see our machine chasing her. About five minutes after we lost sight of her again. The next thing we saw was a bright flame, and we knew that the Zepp

> had been 'strafed'. You should have heard the cheering. Goodness knows where all the voices came from. It was a grand sight from start to finish. Half an hour later the pilot came back. He could hardly speak for excitement. Of course, our boys cheered him till they were hoarse.[4]

By 1917 the rate of loss among the Zeppelins was such that the Germans ceased using them in raids against Britain. They had, however, also developed long-range Gotha bombers and continued their air offensive with these machines. On 7 July 1917 for example twenty-two Gothas made a daylight raid London and the Thanet coast, and there was a terrific air battle over the Thames Estuary between them and a few British machines. People on Southend front watched the fight, and saw several machines brought down. In this raid 40 civilians were killed in London and 194 injured, while 3 were killed in Thanet. Second Lieutenant J.E.R. Young, RFC, aged 19, was killed near the Nore Light in a brave attack on the raiding Gothas, and his body was not recovered.

Training of pilots up to this point was still somewhat haphazard. Austin B. Fee joined the RFC as an observer, from the Northumberland Fusiliers, in 1917. He was interviewed by three officers who were mainly interested in which college he had attended and which games he had represented it in. He was then posted to No. 2 Officer Cadet Wing at Winchester. Training lasted three months:

> The first month was drilling all the time. Everyone had to drill no matter what they were and what qualifications

> they had. The man next to me was a sergeant major from Mons, but it made no difference. The next two months were passed in studying rotary and stationary engines, aeronautics and photography and after that you were a pilot ... Flying had to be done very early in the morning when you were a beginner because the air was bumpy as the day got warmer and you might dip and smash a wing.[5]

Earlier in the war, Canadian officer Harold Hartney was in training at Norwich. His first flight almost ended in disaster:

> Why I am here to tell the tale I don't know. With five other 'huns', the official nickname for embryo flying officers, we spent the morning checking over the types of guns and scanning through our complicated ground course curriculum. At four in the afternoon my big moment arrived. My pilot. Captain Anstey, was a heavy-set man with probably a hundred hours flying time. But he had his wings up and to me was a hero of heroes. The ship was a Maurice Farman longhorn, one of those early box kites with a control surface out in front as well as in the rear. It had a French Renault air-cooled motor rated at eighty horsepower. The pilot and student sat up in front of the motor some ten feet off the ground between the outriggers supporting the advanced control surface.
>
> How sorry I felt for the small detachment of foot-sloggers at one corner of the field, wearily drilling as I had done for so many months, as we sailed off smoothly

into the sunlight on my first hop. We made several circuits over the airdrome at about a hundred and fifty feet and at a speed of around sixty miles an hour. The approach for the first landing of my life seemed so simple and easy but even I, a complete novice, felt that we were over-shooting the field. I was glad when the pilot opened his throttle again to go on. Off we soared, rising gently over some tents and small wooden buildings at the end of the runway.

Suddenly the right wing went up in a vertical bank and we did a quick spiral down from about a hundred and fifty feet, landing squarely on the two sets of double wheels, perfectly and with hardly a bump. With my best manners I said to my instructor, 'Thanks, that was certainly fine.' He looked at me peculiarly and said, 'Boy, you're damn lucky!' It was not until weeks later that I found out he had stalled the plane, it had spun out of control and I had safely come through the one thing that has killed more students than all other causes combined – a spinning nose dive from low altitude.[6]

Former Eton pupil Second Lieutenant W.H.S. Chance had been commissioned into the Worcestershire Regiment but answered an appeal for more officers to become pilots. He was undergoing training in the early part of 1916:

At Reading we studied engines, air-frames, theory of flying, Morse, and other subjects relative to the training of a pilot. Preparations were being made for the great offensive on the Somme and the R.F.C. was being rapidly expanded.

After six weeks at Reading I was posted to No. 5 Reserve Squadron at Castle Bromwich near Birmingham and I rode home on my newly acquired Red Indian motor bike for a brief leave – very excited at the prospect of actually taking to the air.

The aerodrome at Castle Bromwich was large enough to hold three units – a B.E.2c squadron preparing to go overseas, a flight of Avros and R.E.7s and at the north end the Mess and hutments of No. 5 R.A.S. where we were housed. Initial flying training was carried out in Maurice-Farman biplanes – the 'Longhorn' having a front elevator supported by booms and the 'Shorthorn' with rudder and elevator on the tail-plane. Both models had 70 h.p. air-cooled V-8 Renault engines, and the pilot and pupil sat one behind the other in an open nacelle which extended forward of the planes. The Maurice-Farman was not a difficult plane to fly and at ground level would do its 60 m.p.h.

The first entry in my Log-book reads '29 May 1916. 5.37 p.m. M.F.L.H. 6697. Captain Scott. 19 mins. Partial Control.' Dressed in leather flying coats, wool-lined flying boots, flying helmets and goggles, my instructor and I climbed into the nacelle. Captain Scott repeated the engine-starting formula – 'Switch off, suck in, contact.' The Air mechanic – they were colloquially known as 'Ak-Emmas' – swung the prop, the engine fired, the pilot waved his hand – 'Chocks away' – and

> we were off. It is not easy to recall the sensations of a first flight, sitting in the nose of the nacelle in front of the pilot, but Shorthorns only needed a short run to take off and soon we were circling the aerodrome, flying over Castle Bromwich Church, the railway, and the open fields which surrounded the aerodrome ... Over the next fortnight I put in something over an hour's flying, partly on Longhorns and partly on Shorthorns, and was allowed to hold the controls while we practised landings, flying either in the evenings or early mornings. Pilots' training was being rushed at this period of the war and after nine brief flights and two hours and thirty-one minutes of instruction I was considered fit enough to take off on my first solo.[7]

After a total of three hours and fifty-nine minutes flying he had qualified for his 'Ticket', which entitled him to rank as a certificated pilot. Three weeks after posting to Castle Bromwich, Chance was ordered to No. 47 Squadron at Beverley in Yorkshire, commanded by Major J.G. Small. No. 47 Squadron was equipped with Avros and Armstrong Whitworths, both biplanes. The Avro – later to become and for many years to remain the standard primary 'tutor' of the RAF – was a two seater and was equipped with an 80hp rotary Gnome engine, manufactured in France. The seven-cylinder engine, which revolved round a stationary crankshaft, had automatic inlet valves (which sometimes refused to open) and mechanically operated exhaust valves. There was no means of controlling the speed of the engine and before taking off it was necessary to 'blip' – that is to use the button on the top of the joystick to switch on and off. To protect the propeller of the Avro on landing, a skid jutted out from and was fixed to the axle of the landing wheels. The engine was lubricated with castor oil and it was a well-known characteristic that the centrifugal force of the rotating cylinders would spray out a thin film of oil, some of which blew back on to the pupil and instructor, covering face and goggles alike. Avros were not difficult to fly, provided the engine behaved itself, and were much lighter on the controls than the relatively heavy-handed Maurice-Farmans. Inexperienced pilots were warned to treat the controls with delicacy, as too energetic handling could put the plane into a spin; and at that time the technique of recovering from a spin was not taught. Instead, new pilots were advised to fly with caution and avoid 'stunting'. In two weeks of dual instruction – eleven separate outings – Chance put in nearly two hours of flying and after three more trips – one with Major Small who commanded the squadron – he was thought capable of 'going solo'.

Second Lieutenant H.G. Downing was training at Castle Bromwich the following year and recorded that the intensity of the training left him little time for letter writing. Navigation skills were the order of the day:

> I went on a cross country to a neighbouring aerodrome about 30 miles away this evening and had tea there. On my return journey I ran into a rain storm and got lost. When I came out I found I had wandered in a circle and was back at my original starting place. I thought I had

> just enough petrol, so continued my journey. When about 4 miles from this aerodrome, the engine started to misfire and finally stopped. I was a fair height up, about 1,000 feet and just managed to make the aerodrome, missing some telegraph wires by a few inches, and finally stopping right in front of our mess door.[8]

It was not all work however, and Downing found some time for social interaction, innocent enough in its nature: a Saturday afternoon tea with two well-to-do young local girls.

The RFC expected a high standard of work from its mechanics and attention to detail was essential. Indeed, British ground crew established a reputation that was second to none in the world in this regard. Air Mechanic 2nd Class Syd Roach, then in training in London, wrote to a friend in 1915: 'We get a lot of drillings amongst the engines. They are fine things but require a lot of attention, as every time a machine goes up a life is at stake.'[9]

On first enlisting, RNAS Air Mechanic Henry Albert Marsh recalled that he and other 'youngsters' were given a 'shocking' lecture on the horrors of venereal disease from a surgeon commander. Further colour was added afterwards by the petty officer, who warned them in no uncertain terms to stay away from a local prostitute named Millbrook Annie. Air mechanics underwent training at various establishments. H. Owen of Coventry wrote,

> The old Clerget rotary engines brought back memories to me of when I was undergoing a course of technical

> training at Cranwell as a Boy in the old Royal Flying Corps in 1917. I still have recollections of the pungent smell of the burnt pure Castor Oil as it was thrown out into the atmosphere. These engines, revolving around a stationary crankshaft, having no Scavenger system, made us look like spotted leopards after a short run. But nevertheless I was always extremely fascinated, and later on in India I had the first Bentley rotary engine which was more or less a combination of the French engines but produced a much increased horsepower. It was ideal in the old Sopwith machines.[10]

The RAF upon formation had a rank of Boy, to which under age recruits could be appointed. Frank H. Clark, born in September 1900, held this rank when transferred to the RAF in April 1918. Of his previous RFC service with No. 5 Training Depot Station (TDS), he wrote,

> I joined the Royal Flying Corps as a cadet (in 1917). Eventually I was posted to Stamford, where I had some happy days. I was billeted out with a Mrs Gulson, in Burley Lane Cottages. I remember the workshop where engine repairs were done which was a commandeered garage. And on the other side of the lane was a mobile lorry (workshop). Our engine test beds were fixed in Burghley Park. Billeted with me was Corporal F. Winship and Mrs Gulson really mothered us. There was a small number of American Air Force men attached to us for instruction on aircraft engines. We used to

> watch (with amusement) their antics on command from the sergeant – 'into form get, left face, go', and when they returned after lunch the command was 'Stop, disperse to workshop.' Now the airfield was at a small village, Collyweston if I remember rightly. There was nothing to do there so one or two of us usually went to the church Vicarage and played cards with the vicar's wife and daughter. Some pleasant times.[11]

John Dunford had been fascinated by aeroplanes as a boy, after seeing an aerobatic display. Early in 1917 he found himself, much to his astonishment, a member of the RFC. It seemed to him that in that grim year everybody who could breathe and stand upon two legs was being drafted into the infantry, and three months later were in the trenches in France. So, when he found himself as No. 69969 air mechanic RFC he could scarcely believe his luck. However, during the early months he was stationed firstly at Farnborough, the depot of the RFC, and latterly at No. 2 Aircraft Acceptance Park, initially as air mechanic 3rd class but later as a corporal clerk:

> As I and a bunch of other 18 year olds tumbled out of the train at Farnborough station on that cold winter day we were met with a reception committee of two military policemen and a bellowing corporal. It suddenly dawned on me, with some horror, that I was no longer a civilian. We were marched to some cheerless and in hospitable barracks named Malplaquet and allocated a bed. The next night I found that my bed was occupied by another

> new recruit. As I stood in a doorway sheltering from a biting wind and sleet, someone shouted, 'Fall in all men without beds.' I fell in. We were then given two blankets and marched to a cold and draughty concert hall where we slept on the floor, with the wind howling in from every nook and cranny. The next night we were put under canvas on a bleak hillside – 12 men to a tent. [Farnborough] in the days when I was there was infested with military police, disciplinarian NCOs, bellowing sergeant majors and similar unpleasant characters. And it didn't add to my joys when, on cold winter mornings we were taken to the baths at Aldershot and made to plunge into the freezing water.[12]

Eventually Dunford's circumstances changed:

> … after a short period at Farnborough (then the RFC depot) I was posted to Hendon aerodrome, considered the best of all home stations, because it was on the doorstep of London. One couldn't ask for more. In a short time, again more by luck than merit, I was promoted to NCO in charge of test and dispatch, and as such was in a position to get in a lot of flying time with the test pilots. Hendon was designated as an Aircraft Acceptance Park, new machines being received from the manufacturers. Guns were fitted and timed, compass adjusted, and the planes were flight tested before being flown either to Expeditionary Force in France or to mobilising squadrons in the UK. On a test flight it was

necessary to 'loop the loop' several times to make sure that the wings didn't break off. It would have been rather unfortunate if they had, for in those days there were no parachutes or ejector seats.

Actually no wings ever broke off, although there were occasional engine failures resulting in crashes and deaths. The main types of machines then being tested at Hendon were DH4's, DH5's, and DH9's and DH9a's. The DH5 was a single-seater fighter, and the others were reconnaissance planes and capable of carrying small bombs at a cruising speed of 100mph. There was also a DH6 trainer plane which, on full throttle, could attain a speed of 60 mph. In a strong wind I've known these machines to literally 'stand still' in flight. Later, a twin-engined Handley Page came into operation as the main bomber, and, wonder of wonders, during 1918 a four-engined HP made its appearance. This was the first plane with a gun mounted in a rear cockpit. Up till then, the enemy had only to get into the 'blind spot' below the tail and one couldn't fire on him without damaging one's own machine. The four-engined Handley-Page had been designed to bomb Berlin. However this never came about because the war ended soon after the final trials were completed. Indeed, the prototype crashed on its final test flight, killing all 20 occupants – and an unfortunate man on his allotment.[13]

One of the most dangerous tasks performed by air mechanics was swinging a propeller. Private 2nd Class J. Webb was hit by an Avro 504K propeller and sustained a broken arm and leg, resulting in a two-month stay at Prees Heath Military Hospital and a further two months in the camp hospital. Later, when he was posted to operational squadrons, he was excused prop swinging. In 1918 Air Mechanic W.K. Turner of Leeds was based at Netheravon, in Wiltshire with No. 8 TDS. He remembered,

> When the pilot was seated and had checked the ailerons and rudders, a little dialogue ensued – Mechanic: 'Petrol on, switch off, suck in Sir.' Pilot: 'Petrol orn, switch is orf, suck in.' The mechanic would then give the two bladed prop a few turns in the direction of engine rotation and then call 'Contact Sir'. On receiving the reply 'Contact' he would grasp the horizontal propeller facing him on the right hand side near the tip and standing as clear as possible, give it a mighty swing and move quickly backwards … some wouldn't swing props if they could help it and others never really learned how to. Trapped fingers and broken wristwatches often happened and if the engine backfired one had to sense it immediately.[14]

He recalled that one unfortunate air mechanic had a habit of ducking his head forward as he swung the blade. He was warned repeatedly about it, but eventually he was killed by a propeller.

Other Ranks learned on the job, from more senior NCOs. Also, however, they occasionally received classroom-based training. The Regent Street Polytechnic, now part of the

University of Westminster, trained nearly 1,000 air mechanics in the theory of engine magnetos, and riggers went to classes to learn the theory of flight, which was advantageous in that they then knew why an aircraft stays in the air. The wartime expansion of the RFC led to overcrowding, and sometimes insanitary conditions. At Reading, the RFC took over the Jam Factory at Coley Park for the training of recruits, but the facility had a poor reputation; food was notoriously bad and medical care inadequate. Its correct title was the School of Technical Training (Men) and in common with other RFC establishments there was a strong emphasis on physical training. A sports day in May 1917 was held in brilliant weather; events included the long jump, athletics events and boxing:

> There was a very large attendance, including many ladies. Everything went without a hitch ... The comedy element was introduced by two Royal Flying Corps men, dressed as clowns, mounted on donkeys, and armed with bladders ... The performances of the Royal Flying Corps Orchestra, under Second Lieutenant Bower, were much appreciated. Hearty cheers were given for Lieutenant-Colonel Wilford, who distributed the prizes. In the evening there was dancing on the grass.[15]

RFC training policy evolved as the war went on. Through the practice of resting pilots by rotating them from the front back through the training centres, then back to the front and repeating the process, pilots were bringing home experience, giving it to new recruits as trainers, and then returning again to France to accrue more skills.

Major Robert Smith-Barry is sometimes seen as the saviour of the British pilot training system. In 1917 he was given control of the Flying School at Gosport. His approach reflected the fact that his predecessors had been too conservative in their attitude to training pilots. He encouraged trainees to throw their aeroplanes around the sky – indeed he expected the trainers to make sure their pupils did just that. It was his belief that when pilots got to France, the best way to ensure confidence in themselves, and their machine was to have pushed it to the limit in training. Originally, flight training had taught pupils little about why an aeroplane behaved as it did; 'by the book' instruction drilled students on what dangerous manoeuvres to avoid. By contrast, the Gosport System taught the dynamics of flight, and how to apply that knowledge when in the cockpit. For example, earlier pupils had been simply warned to avoid spins; those of 1918 were taught how to get into a spin and then recover from it. Smith-Barry also believed in training the trainer. He came up with a set of criteria for trainers themselves to follow, so that pupils received a standardised set of training.

John Arthur Wilson from Consett, County Durham had already gained the Military Medal with the Machine Gun Corps in France when he transferred to the RAF in April 1918. In September 1918 he became a flight cadet and was posted to No. 6 School of Military Aeronautics at RAF Hastings. He remembered many years later that basic discipline was fierce:

> We were billeted in the big hotel on the main front, in front of the swimming pool at Hastings, the Queen's. What we got was military training; we used to go on the front and take charges, take a whole squadron and turn them. You got Topography that was local map reading, not general map reading, it was local. And Morse Code. But he was a right brute this Commanding Officer [CO], he'd lost his arm, he was an army captain, he was in charge of the hotel, the cadets there. In all my time in the army I never came across anything like that Cadet School at Hastings. The Military Police had you for the slightest thing …[16]

In an attempt to improve both bombing and navigational training, the RFC had recognised that it could learn from the RNAS, which was further advanced in these areas. As a result of deliberations on how to deliver this training, on 5 January 1918 No. 1 School of Navigation and Bomb Dropping came into being at Stonehenge in Wiltshire. Resources were made available by the disbandment of the RFCs No. 2 TDS and the transfer of the RNAS Handley Page Training Squadron. By the time of the Armistice a second such school had been established at Andover, a third in Egypt and a fourth was being established at Andover.

The most ambitious plan of all came in 1917 and 1918 when the RFC began an unprecedented flying training programme in Canada. As aircraft became more vital to waging war, Britain required greater numbers of airmen. In late 1916, expansion plans for the RFC called for the creation of thirty-five new training squadrons. Most would have to be located outside of

Britain, where it was difficult to find space for more airfields and aircraft factories. These requirements led to the Canadian training programme of the latter war years.

As early as December 1914 Canadians had begun to enter the RFC and the RNAS, some by enlistment in Canada, most by transfers from the Canadian Expeditionary Force (CEF). The Canadian entries had commenced as a trickle; by late 1916 they had become a steady stream. The Canadian government did not hinder British recruiting efforts in that country but neither did it do anything to promote aviation. Faced with this official apathy, yet anxious to secure Canadian resources for the RFC, British authorities undertook matters themselves.

The Imperial Munitions Board (IMB), located in Canada and staffed largely by Canadians but directed by the British government, organised the production of armaments for Britain. The IMB secured land for airfields in southern Ontario, constructed barracks and hangars, and established Canadian Aeroplanes Ltd to manufacture Curtiss JN-4 training aircraft. The JN-4s flown in Canada carried a variety of colourful and distinctive markings including maple leaves, terriers, black cats, shamrocks and Jolly Roger insignia. Some were named after cities such as Edmonton and Montreal; at least six bore names commemorating battles of the War of 1812.

Lieutenant Colonel C.G. Hoare, the RFC officer who headed the new training organisation in Canada, moved quickly when he arrived in January 1917. He ordered that flying instruction commence at Long Branch on 28 February 1917, although buildings were still under construction and the first JN-4s had only just been completed and approved for service. The largest school, Camp Borden, began flying training on 30 March 1917. Thereafter, the program mushroomed. By the end of the war there were facilities at Hamilton (Armament School), Toronto (School of Military Aeronautics, recruiting depots), Long Branch (cadet ground training), Beamsville (School of Aerial Fighting), Armour Heights (pilot training, School of Special Flying to train instructors), Leaside (pilot training, Artillery Cooperation School), Camp Rathbun, Deseronto (pilot training), Camp Mohawk, Deseronto (pilot training) and Camp Borden (pilot training). The quarters occupied included public school buildings, a prison and much of the University of Toronto. Camp Borden alone had accommodation for 122 officers, 496 cadets and 1,014 other ranks. The name also changed to Royal Air Force Canada (RAFC) in April 1918.

The Canadian programme trained recruits to basic level, where pilots were almost ready to participate in combat. Finishing touches would be applied at advanced schools in Britain or France. The training in Canada grew more sophisticated as instructional staff gained experience, the RFC provided details of improved methods being developed in Britain, and units at the front sent 'feedback' about how new aircrew could be better prepared. The most important changes came with the adoption by 1918 of the Gosport System, developed by Smith-Barry.

William Hector Ptolemy was a typical trainee. An instructor took him up for a brief introductory flight, at No. 88 Canadian Training Squadron (CTS), Armour Heights, on 3 December 1917. He took the controls for the first time during a twenty-five-minute flight two days later. Bad weather occasionally interrupted his training and on 16 December 1917 he broke a propeller while landing in snow. He smashed another propeller on 22 December, and generally had difficulty with turns. On 3 January 1918, he flew for forty minutes, executed seven landings and made an emergency landing when his engine failed. He reported his first landing on skis on 29 January. Finally, on 5 February, having flown seven hours and twenty-five minutes with an instructor, he made his first solo circuits; most pupils soloed after five hours.

Thereafter, Ptolemy regularly flew alone. His terse logbook entries hint at his excitement; on 11 February 1918 he was airborne seventy minutes and described the trip as 'Up to Newmarket – went for a joyride'. In mid-February he moved to the training squadrons at Leaside where more advanced manoeuvres were taught, notably formation flying and the first aerial photography exercises. On 10 April 1918, he first reported dropping bombs. He subsequently attended the School of Aerial Gunnery at Beamsville for a brief advanced course in gunnery and photography before being posted overseas. After further advanced training in Britain and France he reported to No. 201 Squadron, which was equipped with Sopwith Camel fighter aircraft, on 4 October 1918. Following the war, he became a bush pilot.

With little experience in severe cold weather flying, the RFC authorities feared that training might be shut down entirely for the winter of 1917 to 1918. As a result, a large portion of the program was relocated to Fort Worth, Texas, where the organisation also trained many Americans and exchanged information on training methods with the United

States flying services. Meanwhile, the training squadrons that remained in Canada that winter fitted their JN-4s with skis, worked out special cold-weather formulas for lubricants and kept the system operating at least as well as the organisation in Texas, where mud proved as frustrating as deep snow.

Overall, the training scheme enrolled 9,200 cadets. Of these, 3,135 completed pilot training and more than 2,500 were sent overseas; the balance of graduates were either retained as instructors or were awaiting postings to Britain when the Armistice was signed. In addition, 137 observers graduated of whom 85 were sent overseas. The program also turned out at least 7,400 mechanics. A number of American personnel, both navy and army, were trained in Canada, as were four or five White Russians.

The results were achieved at some cost. At least 129 cadets and some 20 instructors were killed in flying accidents, although the safety record did improve. In April 1917, there was one fatality for every 200 hours flown; in December 1917, one fatality for every 1,500 hours, and in October 1918, one fatality for every 5,800 hours flown. The most publicised accident of the program involved no injuries: a JN-4, attempting a forced landing on Oshawa's main street on 22 April 1918, became entangled with telephone wires and pinned near the top of a large store front, where it remained suspended for several hours.

One of the instructors was Captain Geoffrey H. Bonnell, who had served with No. 32 Squadron RFC from July to December 1916, flying the DH.2. He was an American of Canadian descent, who began the war as a gunner in the Canadian

Field Artillery. By the time Bonnell left his squadron, he had advanced to acting flight commander and the rank of captain. Bonnell's reputation preceded him because many people gave him credit for bringing down Oswald Boelcke. This story was false but it elevated Bonnell's stature because Boelcke was one of Germany's most famous fighter pilots, the father of organised fighter tactics, and the Red Baron's tutor. Bonnell was part of the initial cadre assigned to the RFC training complex at Toronto. He established a solid reputation, according to his superior, as 'one of the few excellent officers in Canada.'[17] His record and American citizenship made him an ideal candidate for transfer to the United States Air Service (USAS). He became a major in the United States Army Signal Corps on 3 October 1917.

The first women who could reasonably claim to have served with the air arm in the First World War were motor transport drivers who had enlisted in 1916 into the Women's Legion and had then been attached to the RFC. They were allowed to wear suitably adapted RFC uniforms and badges. These women had to be confident in their technical ability as well as driving skills, as they had full responsibility for their vehicle and its maintenance. Upon the formation of the RAF in April the Women's Royal Air Force (WRAF) was created from the Women's Legion, as well as elements of the Women's Royal Naval Service (WRNS) and Queen Mary's Army Auxiliary Corps (QMAAC). The principal aim of the WRAF was to train women to take over the work of home-based mechanics, and so free them for service in the combat areas.

The minimum age for enlistment was 18 and the women had to produce two references: one of which had to be from a woman who had known them for at least two years and could attest to their character. There were two categories to which a woman could be posted: mobile (liable to serve in any part of the United Kingdom) and immobile (once trained to serve only in their home town or locality). A curious fact of the pay structure was that the highest paid trade was that of a shorthand typist, all other trades being lower on a sliding scale until at the bottom was the lowly general domestic worker. In the beginning, recruits were enlisted through the local Labour Exchange and were employed on civilian contracts. This anomaly created some problems with discipline. When, after the Armistice, some women were posted to France they came under the Air Force Act, which made discipline much more effective. Control was also enforced via the WRAF Patrol. This was effectively a form of military police identified by the dark blue armband, which its members wore. The WRAF patrol policed camps and public places frequented by servicewomen. They were not allowed to drink or smoke in bars, nor could they be seen 'loitering'.

Some of the trades that involved working on aeroplanes included that of rigger – usually taught by RAF riggers on an 'on-the-job' basis. Wire or cable splicing was carried out under supervision on actual aircraft. Recruits who proved particularly adept were allowed to work on dismantling damaged aircraft unsupervised. Aero engine fitters were restricted to cleaning parts after an engine had been stripped but again, particularly efficient recruits might help to reassemble an engine. Painters and dopers were permitted to work in all-female workshops.

Chapter Three

Western Front, 1915–1916

The first winter of the war had revealed addition problems associated with cold weather maintenance of aeroplanes. Aside from the difficulties of working on metal at low temperatures with chilled hands, which could make the task of a couple of hours last all day, radiators froze and the castor oil of rotary engines degenerated into a gum, which clogged pipes and channels. Greases hardened, dope and varnish thickened. The only form of heating was coke braziers that offered a potential fire hazard in closed hangars. At altitude, machine guns suffered similarly from congealed oil, jamming or refusing to fire. Bombs refused to release from frozen mechanisms. Ice-hardened ground damaged the fragile undercarriages of the aircraft. The technology of operating an air force in active service conditions in winter was in its infancy, and indeed some of these problems would not be resolved through four more years of war.

Flight Lieutenant Harold Rosher was at this point with No. 1 Naval Squadron at Dunkirk. On 7 March 1915, he took part in a raid on the German submarine base at Ostend. At this early stage in the war his letters have a naïve quality – on a day's leave he and a fellow pilot took passports and motored off in a car to Belgium to 'see the war'. A puncture in a tyre put paid to their planned tourist excursion, though they were assisted in changing the tyre by a group of Belgian soldiers anxious to show their gratitude to anyone English for the help that their country had received in the war so far. However as the weeks went by, and more air casualties were reported or witnessed, the letters betrayed a growing sense of concern for his own safety, alternating with fatalistic thoughts. On 23 March 1915, he wrote,

> Have spent a very busy day tuning up my bus, and am not over satisfied with it now. Tomorrow at the crack of dawn I am off on another stunt, this time more hazardous than ever. When I start thinking of the possibilities, or rather probabilities, I go hot and cold by turns; so endeavour to switch off on to something else, but it keeps coming back to the same old thing.

The following day, 24 March 1915, he took part in a raid on the submarine base at Hoboken, near Antwerp, attacking U-boats under construction, and his next letter is full of elation both at his achievement and the fact that he survived to tell the tale:

> Last night we slept at the aerodrome, so as to get off at the 'crack of dawn'. This morning we got up about 3.30a.m. (thank goodness, the weather was warm), and breakfast followed. It's mighty hard to get down eggs and bread and butter at that hour. We cut for the order of starting, but decided to keep as near one another as possible. I went off last but one, at 5.30a.m., and streaked out straight across the sea. We were pretty heavily loaded,

and my bus wouldn't climb much. I saw one machine ahead of me, but lost it almost immediately in the clouds, which were very low (2,500 feet), and it was also very misty.

Our course was right up the coast, past Zeebrugge, and then cut in across the land. At the mouth of the Scheldt I got clear of some of the clouds and saw Courtney behind and 2,000 feet above me, my machine then being about 5,000 feet only. He rapidly overtook me (we were all on Avros, but his was faster), and from then on I followed him over the clouds. Unfortunately, over Antwerp there were no clouds. Courtney was about five or six minutes in front of me, and I saw him volplane out of sight. I had to go on some little way before I spotted the yards myself. I next saw Courtney very low down, flying away to the coast with shrapnel bursting around him. He came down to under 500 feet, and being first there, dropped his bombs before he was fired on.

As the wind was dead against me, I decided to come round in a semi-circle to cross the yards with the wind, so as to attain a greater speed. I was only 5,500 feet up, and they opened fire on me with shrapnel as soon as I got within range. It began getting a bit hot, so before I got quite round I shut off my petrol, and came down with a steep volplane until I was 2,500 feet, when I turned on my petrol again, and continued my descent at a rate of well over a hundred miles an hour. I passed over the yards at about 1,000 feet only, and loosed all my bombs over the place. The whole way down I was under fire, two

> anti-aircraft in the yard, guns from the forts on either side, rifle fire, mitrailleuse or machine guns, and, most weird of all, great bunches (15 to 20) of what looked like green rockets, but I think they were flaming bullets. The excitement of the moment was terrific. I have never travelled so fast before in my life. My chief impressions were the great speed, the flaming bullets streaking by, the incessant rattle of the machine gun and rifle fire, and one or two shells bursting close by, knocking my machine all sideways, and pretty nearly deafening me … I found myself across the yards, and felt a mild sort of surprise. My eyes must have been sticking out of my head like a shrimp's!
>
> I know I was gasping for breath and crouching down in the fuselage. I was, however, by no means clear, for shrapnel was still bursting around me. I jammed the rudder first one way and then the other. I banked first on to one wing tip, and then on to the other, now slipping outwards, and now up and now down. I was literally hedged in by forts (and only 1,000 feet up), and had to run the gauntlet before getting away. I was under rifle fire right up to the frontier, and even then the Dutch potted me.[1]

Amazingly, back at his base, he found that his machine had been hit only twice, with one bullet hole through the tail and a piece of shrapnel buried in the main spar of one wing. Captain Ivon T. Courtney, RMLI who commanded the raid had arrived in Belgium in late August 1914, with other aircrew from

Eastchurch, to form the nucleus of the naval wing guarding the Channel ports. In the raid on Hoboken he succeeded in dropping four bombs from 1,000ft on the boats and works. He was remembered as a dashing and good-looking officer, who wore an unofficial blue uniform of his own design, which his contemporaries copied and which became the model for the later Royal Marine officers' 'B serge' uniform. He died aged 93 in 1978.

In May 1915, Sub-Lieutenant Rex Warneford joined No. 1 Wing RNAS at Veurne on the Belgian coast. Over the next few weeks, Warneford was involved in attacks on German troops and guns, as well as actions against enemy aircraft. His aggressiveness and effectiveness led to his being given his own aeroplane and a roving commission. On 17 May 1915, Warneford encountered a Deutsches Heer-flown Zeppelin airship, LZ 39, setting out on a raid over the United Kingdom. He attacked LZ 39 with machine gun fire but the airship was able to ascend out of range by jettisoning ballast. On 7 June 1915 at Ghent, Belgium, Warneford, flying a Morane-Saulnier Type L, attacked another German army airship, LZ 37. He chased the airship from the coast near Ostend and, despite its defensive machine-gun fire, succeeded in dropping his six 20lb Hale bombs on it, the last of which set the airship on fire. LZ 37 subsequently came down in Sint-Amandsberg, Ghent, where it crashed into a convent school, killing two nuns. The commander of LZ 37, Oberleutnant Otto van der Haegen, and seven members of the crew were also killed. The explosion overturned Warneford's aircraft and stopped its engine in mid-air. Having no alternative, Warneford had to land behind enemy lines, but after thirty-five minutes spent on repairs, he managed to restart the engine just as the Germans realised what was going on, and after yelling 'Give my regards to the Kaiser!', he was able to get the machine airborne and returned to base. For this action, Warneford was awarded the Victoria Cross (VC), but did not live to wear it, for he was killed in a flying accident a few days later.

This was the first destruction of a German airship by a British airman. It could be argued that the front line of the air defence of the United Kingdom was actually here in Belgium with the concerted efforts of the RNAS to attack and destroy the Zeppelins either in the air, or in their sheds and hangars. For the RFC, the enemy airships were also an occasional target; Captain Lanoe Hawker of No. 6 Squadron records, in a letter, dropping bombs on a Zeppelin shed while using an enemy kite balloon as cover from ground fire – a feat that earned him the DSO. Yet for the men and machines of the RFC in France, first and foremost their priority was the support of ground operations by the army. The Battle of Neuve Chapelle, in March 1915, had seen the first concerted attempt to systematically photograph the battlefield of a planned offensive in advance. Key targets such as enemy headquarters and railway yards had been identified from the air and had then been subjected to artillery bombardment.

For most of 1915, the workhorse of the RFC on such operations would be the pre-war B.E.2; the two seater was ubiquitous and used for these and a range of other duties. It had been steadily improved in its various marques, and had enjoyed some success, but was now outclassed. The presence on the Western Front of the superior Fokker E.1 *Eindecker*, with its interrupter gear and forward firing machine guns had caused casualties in numbers, which were impossible to ignore. These were the days of the so-called Fokker Scourge. In these early months of aerial combat, two-seater squadrons on reconnaissance operations were also routinely equipped with one or two single seater scouts with some form of armament, to act not merely as fast reconnaissance aircraft, but to provide protection against enemy machines. However, the first successful purpose-built British single seat fighter, the de Havilland DH.2 'pusher' was on the way, and would soon begin to equip British squadrons in France. It was this machine more than any other that would gradually turn the tide against the Fokker and force the Germans to introduce new models in the battle for aerial supremacy.

In June 1915, Captain Robert Maxwell Pike of No. 5 Squadron RFC was recalled to Hendon to test fly the prototype of the new machine. He reported that it had potential:

> I found that she climbed exceedingly well and is apparently capable of a climb to 3500 feet fully loaded in well under 5 minutes. The speed without streamlined wires is about 85 miles per hour. The machine was flying a little nose heavy and the tail fin had not been adjusted to counteract the torque, also there was a good deal of vibration which I believe to be due to engine and propeller being out of balance. There were a few main alterations to be made. I strongly advise wing skids and drift wires to the front of the nacelle which should

> prevent vibration of the instrument board. Also the fin required to be put well over and a slight alteration be made to the tail plane. Even without these alterations, which will make the machine more comfortable to fly, she will be of enormous value out here. With practice one should be able to use the gun effectively and the range of fire is very large, and the vision greater than any other machine I have flown.[2]

It was now felt that active service evaluation of the DH.2 prototype was needed, and astonishingly, on 26 July 1915, this sole example of the machine was given serial No. DH.2 4732 and sent to France under the command of No. 5 Squadron, RFC, based at that point at St Omer. The potential risks of this move appear not to have been considered at the time. On 9 August 1915, Captain Robert Maxwell Pike again took the prototype into the air and was on a patrol in the vicinity of Ypres, Belgium. The mission took a turn for the worse when he became embroiled in a dogfight with an Albatros two seater, piloted by Abteilungsfürer Alfred Ritscher with his air gunner Leutnant Heinrich Maas of the German navy. Pike received a mortal wound to the head but was able to land behind enemy lines just east of Ypres, though the aeroplane somersaulted in rough ground. The loss of the prototype was a potential disaster to the British, and the worst consequences were feared. Fortunately, the Germans, though they repaired the aeroplane showed little curiosity, and made no attempt at a full and detailed examination. They thereby left it to their own flyers over the next year to discover for themselves what the DH.2 was really capable of. The Germans meanwhile informed the British of Pike's death by means of an air drop, piloted by Theo Osterkamp. The message stated, 'The gallant Captain Pike was shot down in mortal combat and was buried in a churchyard behind our lines with full military honours.'[3]

Pike was buried beneath an ornately constructed wooden cross in a local churchyard, though his grave was later lost. His name is now recorded on the Arras Flying Services Memorial.

The Germans were also keen to photograph British positions wherever possible, and later that year a new type of Albatros machine was shot down behind British lines by Corporal Thomas Bennett, RFC; it landed more or less intact, and was found to be carrying three cameras. Bennett, from Battersea, London had been one of the first airmen to reach France in 1914. He had been with the RFC since enlisting in 1912, and he gave his trade as motor mechanic when signing his papers; he had been in action since the Retreat from Mons, but displayed characteristic reticence when interviewed by a journalist about the exploits that had earned him the Distinguished Conduct Medal (DCM). He stated that it was all in a day's work, and when asked how it felt to be up in the air when German anti-aircraft guns were 'potting' at the plane, he said that really there was so much to do that one had no time to feel nervous or do anything but attend to the work at hand. The great speed of the aeroplane, 70 or 80mph, made it imperative for attention to be concentrated if any reliable information was to be gained from reconnaissance work, and when added to this the fact that the gun had to be operated to prevent the attention of enemy aircraft, then every second was occupied in attending to business. In the earlier stages of the war, he continued, the German aeroplanes were continually coming over the British lines, but latterly that had changed, and now as a rule the German flying men kept within their own borders, so that if they were brought down the machine nearly always fell in territory that was under German occupation. He also stated that the Germans would seldom attack a British machine unless the odds were in their favour, indeed they would never engage an Allied aeroplane unless it was at least three or four to one in their favour. The report continued,

> Corporal Bennett's Distinguished Conduct Medal was won on September 13th [1915], when Lieutenant Shield and he were on patrol work. They had an air fight with a German Albatros which they finally disabled, and which fell to the south of the British lines. The official account says they engaged at a height of 7,000 feet, and 'Corporal Bennett handled his gun with great coolness and skill, and succeeded in disabling the German machine, which side-slipped, nose-dived, and came to ground in our lines.' The two German aviators were killed. Lieutenant Shield received the Military Cross for participation in this fight.[4]

The incident took place over the Bois de Bicz; the pair flying in a B.E.2c from No. 16 Squadron. Both Bennett and Lieutenant Horace Shield escaped without injury in this contest but about a month later Bennett, whilst again on patrol work was hit in the elbow by a shell from an anti-aircraft gun. After three weeks in a French infirmary he was brought to Leicester Base Hospital, where some further operations were necessary, but it was hoped that he would regain full use of his arm. The article concluded,

> He has received a number of congratulatory letters from the officers of his unit, expressing the hope that he will soon be able to go back to duty, and that is his own wish, for he is very keen on the work, and was well on the way to promotion when he sustained the injury.

A great deal of development had taken place in the RFC between the Battle of Neuve Chapelle in March 1915 and the Battle of Loos in September 1915. Loos was the biggest air battle fought to that date, and represented the point at which the RFC might be said to have moved from making a small but useful contribution to operations on the Western Front to becoming an integral part of the BEF's activities. Up to now, a lack of suitable wireless equipment had delayed progress. Wireless sets were heavy, and it was beyond the capability of the RFC's aircraft to carry both a wireless set and an observer to operate it. While it was possible for pilots to both fly and observe for the fall of shot, this was not ideal. Now, the arrival of the Sterling Spark wireless in 1915 solved the problem of weight, but availability was a different matter; it took quite some time for the new wireless set to be installed across the RFC.

The Sterling Spark gap wireless transmitter, also referred to as the No. 1 Aircraft Transmitter Spark, was the first purpose-built airborne wireless set used by the RFC in the First World War. The transmitter and Morse key were totally enclosed to avoid a spark igniting the petrol vapour in the aircraft cockpit. The set was designed for airborne reconnaissance using Morse code, most commonly artillery spotting working with British Army artillery stations on the Western Front but also for spotting German U-boats at sea. Communication was in one direction only so the sender, usually the observer in a two-person biplane, had no way of knowing if the message had been received or not. Nonetheless, the set was very useful indeed with later examples having a transmitter and receiver.

Another new machine just reaching the front line at this time was the Vickers FB5 Gunbus. In November 1915, No. 18 Squadron RFC, equipped with this machine, moved to France. Before leaving Britain, each of the squadron's riggers and fitters had been sent for a week's course at Vickers' works at Crayford, Kent, to learn details of its manufacture and maintenance. After two months of this familiarisation the squadron was deployed to the front; initially it was as a mobile unit and was often under fire from German long-range guns. It then had to dismantle hangars and gear and be on the move within four hours, move 30 miles to a new site, erect the hangars and have the aeroplanes ready for dawn patrol the next morning. This nomadic lifestyle meant that for groundcrew on this squadron life was rough. Often accommodation was basic, with mechanics sometimes sleeping on the floor of the hangar. Latrines would be a long trench with a pole above, which required a degree of balance to use without mishap or cut-down petrol tins.

In spring 1916 this squadron was re-equipped with F.E.2bs, which mounted the powerful 120hp Beardmore engine. No. 11 Squadron would also re-equip with these machines later in the year, but it was in an F.B.5 that Air Mechanic 2nd Class Ernest Coleman, an observer from this squadron flying with Second Lieutenant J.S. Castle as pilot took part in a photo reconnaissance mission in March 1916. The greatest fear for aircrew, given the flammable materials of which their machines were constructed and the fragile nature of their fuel tanks, was fire. Aircrew were known to carry revolvers in order to shoot themselves if a machine caught fire, rather than be burned to death, or to jump rather than be incinerated. An extraordinary account illustrating this survives from Coleman, who wrote later,

> I heard from Mr Castle that his engine was hit and he was forced to land. We were going down all speed but the fire continued and anything flammable began to burn. I saw no time to strip my gun, so unfastened it and threw it out in one piece, feeling rather sorry for whoever it should fall upon. Then I had my camera which I also flung over the side but it was so light that it passed between the top and bottom planes and struck the propeller – which it evidently broke as the remainder of the descent was accompanied by terrible engine vibration … I burnt my maps, which was rather easy as it only necessitated placing my map case near the flame and the celluloid caught the lot at once, I was expecting the machine to get out of control any moment or the tail to catch fire.

> Fortunately neither of these happened but I was prepared for the worst and with my legs hanging over the side I was ready to leap for it. This I was seriously thinking of doing, as everything was beginning to burn and the only thing that stopped me from catching alight was my keeping across the top of the nacelle and not in it.
>
> Mr Castle saw I had intentions of leaping out as I looked round to see if he was alright and keeping control. He motioned me to remain. You can imagine what Mr Castle's plight had been all this while, the flames were burning his face and the heat and flames were nearly suffocating him; also petrol was running under the nacelle and forming a burning pool at the rudder controls. It was this that accounted for his foot being burned, yet with all this he was fine and kept quite cool, not losing his head but struggling to land her safely. Writing all this sounds that we were a long time coming down, but the actual time was somewhere about a minute and our height when hit 8,600 feet. I do not know how Mr Castle stuck it – he was a marvel and I cannot find words to express his coolness and admirable conduct during the whole engagement. His coolness saved our two lives. About 100 feet Mr Castle managed to flatten out and landed as though he was landing on the aerodrome.[5]

As soon as the machine came to a halt Coleman was out, and shaking Castle's hand to thank him for saving both their lives, but the pilot's flying coat was still alight and he was obviously in great pain. By the time German troops arrived on the scene he had managed to get Castle's coat off. Castle was given medical attention, but the machine now was a burning wreck. For officers at least, the treatment that they could expect when captured was extremely civilised. There was in this war still a 'camaraderie of the air' between opposing airmen, and the Germans in particular were keen to entertain downed British flyers in their mess. The father of Lieutenant W. Baxter-Ellis who had been reported missing around this time, received a letter at his home in Newcastle-upon-Tyne, which had been dropped in the British lines by a German machine. It stated that his son had been brought down by a Fokker on the enemy side of the line, but he was currently being well cared for by two German flying officers.

In June 1916, Canadian pilot Harold Hartney proceeded to France on active service for the first time. He was posted to No. 20 Squadron, based about 8 miles from Cassel. This squadron was in the process of re-equipping with F.E.2d machines, which mounted the new even more powerful Rolls-Royce engine. Straight away he was impressed with the camaraderie he found there. With the officers living closely together at the aerodrome, socialising and fraternising when not on duty, they were soon all of a single mind, which greatly aided teamwork. On his first operational sortie, he encountered the pilot's worst nightmare, an engine seizure on take-off. The standard response to this occurrence, to land straight ahead, was at this stage in the war not yet universal, and so he turned to glide back to the airfield. It was a highly dangerous manoeuvre, which had killed many pilots, but Hartney got away with it. A few days later he was informed at mess in the evening that the following day he would be going on a balloon strafing expedition. His gunner would be a seasoned NCO, Corporal Hodder. That first operational sortie brought his first contact with an 'EA' and with it an interesting sidelight on the relationship between officer pilots and non-commissioned observers:

> I frightened my gunner, Hodder, more than myself as I leaned forward on the controls and to my surprise found myself overtaking the enemy ship. I was about on his tail, close enough to do business when my gunner signalled 'wash-out' (jammed guns or something else making it in-advisable to continue the combat). Being much his junior in minutes in combat over the front (this being my very first second) I slowly broke away but as I did so, our momentum carrying us almost even with him, I could see the trouble.
>
> From the rear cock-pit of the German bi-plane ship an enemy gunner was working his Spandau and bullets were flying past us plenty. The Spandau's cadence of firing was considerably slower than ours. I had lost altitude so much faster than I had been told I would, I had caught him so quickly, I had forgotten about that Boche gunner in the rear cock-pit. I had not co-operated with my gunner. I had risked his life and mine unnecessarily – a dozen things made me ashamed of myself and I felt my whole mission had been a terrible failure...[6]

By now, preparations were being undertaken further south for the forthcoming Battle of the Somme. A large portion of these efforts were being carried out by the men and machines of the

RFC. The strength of the corps on the Somme front had grown progressively during June 1916, and the British Fourth Army now had some 109 aircraft directly in its support plus a further 70 upon which it could call for reinforcement. Opposing them were 129 German aircraft of various types. Allied aerial observation of the German positions was hampered by bad weather that month – on 23 June 1916 lightening destroyed the kite balloons of No. 1 and No. 14 sections and damaged another. On 24 June, in low cloud and rain, the preparatory bombardment for the attack began. Despite the difficulties imposed by the weather, RFC pilots flew low and directed fire onto forty enemy targets. Two days later British aviators made a concerted effort to cripple the German capability for observation, by attacking German observation balloons along the entire front. Five were destroyed, followed by another three on 26 June. Although the main theatre of operations was to the south, for Hartney's squadron this was immaterial. To flyers there was no clear-cut line anywhere, and 15 miles one way or another made little difference. Their task now was to take the fight to the enemy, particularly those aircraft operating from Lille. Now he was with another veteran NCO gunner, Sergeant Stanley, and the squadron was to work in formation, something rarely attempted so far on the Western Front, because of the difficulty in assembling a group of machines of the same specification. After watching a comrade destroy an enemy machine, they were almost jumped by a Fokker *Eindecker* coming at them from above and behind. Hartney reacted fast and performed a blind Immelmann turn to come up behind the enemy scout:

> As the poor fellow went down, Stanley turned around to me with a sickly, half-guilty but triumphant smile below his leather-rimmed face mask and goggles. With one hand he signalled 'thumbs down' for the fallen enemy – a traditional gesture with all war aviators. I banked up and looked over the side for a moment to see where the Fokker hit. Then I came to my senses. We were much further over the enemy lines than we should have been, our gas was running low and we had a nasty head wind to buck. It was time to scuttle for home – a mean job well done. I had killed, or helped to kill, my first German. I could feel no exultation. I could only think of that black clad flyer in flames – and his family.[7]

More German aircraft appeared and after a fierce fight, he was forced down with engine damage into a field behind some support trenches, on the Armentieres-Bailleul road.

> Stanley and I jumped out quickly. 'Right-o, that'll do!' he said and came over and put his arm around me. Then we began to inspect our plane. It was in horrible shape, riddled with bullets and how it held together is a mystery. The fabric in places was torn clear from the leading edge to the trailing. If we had tried to paint an Iron Cross on every hole, as we did later in the war, it would have taken all night. That motor should have been put in a museum. It had saved our lives but how it did it I don't know to this day. Seven bullets were actually sticking in the water jackets and in the plumbing. The cowling

> was almost a sieve. And here's gospel truth, although my word on it has often been doubted – four of the aluminium pistons, a secret Rolls-Royce innovation, had actually fused and were holding up four of the exhaust valves. There was no water whatever in the engine and practically no oil. For those last few minutes it had been doing its bit for old England metal to metal – at melting temperatures. I pulled out two of the bullets and kept them for souvenirs. Stanley, much more experienced than I, merely shook his head, mumbling, 'A miracle! A bloody miracle!'[8]

After contacting their CO to inform him of their location, with infantry help the wrecked machine was removed to Bailleul town square, where they were met by one of the squadron lorries.

British commanders now faced a conundrum. Experience, particularly at the Battle of Loos the previous year, had taught them that if an offensive was to stand any chance of success, then ammunition dumps must be created within easy reach of the front line, and camps must be established in in similar proximity in which to hold reinforcements, ready to quickly exploit any breakthrough. The trouble was that these thorough preparations, necessary though they were, also signalled like a beacon to the enemy the probable location of a forthcoming attack. The Germans for their part could be in no doubt that something was afoot on the Somme front. In spite of British efforts to restrict aerial observation, their pilots could still see and report the developments below them. The only question as far as the Germans were concerned was what to make of all this activity. Indeed, to them, British and French preparations seemed so obvious as to constitute a deliberate feint, at least as far as the army was concerned. German airmen however repeatedly tried to warn their infantry counterparts that a major Anglo-French attack on the Somme was imminent. A senior German air officer wrote of this at the end of the war, stating that,

> In March 1916, our airmen reported the movement of large masses of troops of the French Arras group to the south, numerous new tented camps north of the Somme, and attempts by the enemy airmen to block us and deny us this insight. Thus, for example, the Bavarian Flying Section Nr 1 found on 23 April, to the east of Villers Brettoneux two new enemy airfields, also a large practice works at Corbie, likewise large new factory-like buildings in the same area. By mid-May, the two aforementioned airfields had increased to four, with thirteen sheds for about 50 aircraft, also reported was the emergence of tented and hutted camps between the Ancre and the Somme. Military training areas and railway facilities at Vecquemont were visible in the photos. In the reports the view was also expressed that the camps north of the Somme could be regarded as English and those south of the Somme as of French origin. In May, similar findings were made by Flying Sections 23, 32 and 59. Already by then there could be little doubt about the area and direction of the attack.

In the first half of June, pictures from the area of Hammerwald showed new attack trenches, leading far back from the front to the north. The leader of the Bavarian Flying Section Nr 1 brought this information to the responsible staff officer of the XIV Reserve Armee Korps for discussion, stressing that together with lively and aggressive enemy air activity in this area, it meant that an attack from that direction must be likely … A flight by the same unit on 17 June showed with complete clarity a massive proliferation of battery positions, dugout constructions, proximity, assembly and cable trenches, especially south and east of Hammerwald. All photographic images were rushed to General Headquarters and to the AOK 2 and to the troops concerned. On 19 June, the findings made so far were confirmed by further aerial reconnaissances [*sic*], especially the construction of a honeycomb of trenches in the park and to the south of Maricourt.

On 20 June, General Headquarters was presented with a new sketch showing the position of the recently constructed works. On 17 July on the occasion of my presence at the Bavarian Flying Section Nr 1, I personally had sight of a copy of an aviator's message dated 22 June, 10.30am to the General Headquarters XIV Reserve Armee Korps, endorsed with the following wording: 'The enemy attack – when he attacks – will have Maricourt as the centre of the right wing, not only the area around Gommecourt. He will not miss the Fricourt salient which is tactically favourable to him.'[9]

There was also a noticeable increase in aerial patrols; in the weeks before the attack, efforts had been made to photograph the entire front line faced by the Fourth Army. Some aircraft bombed and harassed German reserves and reinforcements, whilst others attacked enemy observers in kite balloons. In the last days of June, a new British weapon, the Le Prieur rocket, together with phosphorous bombs, were used by the RFC to bring down eight such balloons. Perhaps the most important duty of the allied airmen was counter-battery work, as Captain Alfred J. Evans remembered,

> For over three months No. 3 Squadron had been occupied daily in ranging the heavy guns which night after night crept into their allotted positions in front of Albert. On July 1st 1916 the Somme offensive opened with gas and smoke and a bombardment of unprecedented severity. To the pilots and observers in an artillery squadron the beginning of this battle brought a certain relief, for we were rather tired of flying up and down, being shot at continually by fairly accurate and remarkably well hidden anti-aircraft batteries, while we registered endless guns on uninteresting points. On the German side of the trenches, before the battle, the country seemed almost peaceful and deserted. Anti-aircraft shells arrived and burst in large numbers, coming apparently from nowhere, for it was almost rare to see a flash on the German side; if one did, it was probably a dummy flash; and of movement, except for a few trains in the distance, there was none. Only an expert observer would know

> that the thin straight line was a light railway; that the white lines were paths made by the ration parties and reliefs following the dead ground when they came up at night; that the almost invisible line was a sunken pipe line for bringing water to the trenches, and that the shading which crept and thickened along the German reserve trenches showed that the German working parties were active at night if invisible in the day time. For the shading spelt barbed wire.
>
> Only about half a dozen times during those three months did I have the luck to catch a German battery firing. When that happened one ceased the ranging work and called up something really heavy, for preference a nine-inch howitzer battery, which pulverised the Hun.[10]

However, it must also be stated that the bad weather and cloud in the last two days before the attack seriously interfered with the ability of the RFC to undertake this work. The logbook of observer Captain T. Stallibrass, also with No. 3 Squadron, describes the situation astride the Albert-Bapaume road, on the first day of the Somme offensive:

> A very cloudy morning. As we neared the lines an immense cloud of smoke and dust was hanging over La Boiselle – this being the result of the large mine exploded by British which partly destroyed Hun front line, and formed an enormous crater. Clouds were low, and the crater was gradually hidden by smoke from shells & shrapnel, white smoke drifting – our guns putting up

a heavy barrage which lifted well when timed to do so, right ahead of our infantry. At 7.30am the artillery ceased firing on the Hun front line and our infantry got out of the trenches on a front from Montauban to La Boiselle on the XV Corps front, and from La Boiselle to Thiepval on III Corps front. They could be plainly seen crossing 'no man's land', & falling down under heavy machine gun fire. The noise even from the air was intense.

We flew just behind Hun lines & our barrage. Hun artillery not very active. Archie with complete wind up, & hardly fired at all. The attack on the XV Corps front was very successful. Mametz – Montauban & Fricourt being taken. The III Corps attack failed generally. They lost heavily, & our troops omitted to clear dugouts in La Boiselle & Ovillers-La Boiselle. The Huns came out afterwards & took them in the rear.

Engaged X16 a 19 with 55th Hows [Howitzers]. Also Pozieres main road. Several OPs & some waggons were strafed. Good shoot. Saw the attack on La Boiselle. Our infantry left the trenches at four o'clock [pm], & rushed across 'no man's land'. They reached the trenches headed by an officer, or NCO who was about 10 yards in front. They reached the line & could be seen getting through the wire, & hand to hand fighting with the Hun.[11]

Franz Seldte was a machine gun officer in the nearby German Infanterie Regiment Nr 66. On the morning of 1 July 1916 he was positioned north of Serre. He published his memoirs after the war, a now almost forgotten account in which he refers to himself throughout in the third person as 'Helmut Stahl'. He describes the tension and apprehension of the buildup to the British attack, the barrage, and the nerves as German soldiers wait for the Tommies to come on this beautiful summer's day. He even makes reference to RFC aircraft buzzing low over no man's land. In one of these aeroplanes was another witness to the events taking place here. This was Lieutenant Edward Packe of No. 15 Squadron RFC, flying as an observer in a two-seater B.E.2c, with his cockpit in front of that of the pilot. He was on reconnaissance on the morning of the attack, and found the Germans in a hostile mood, writing in his diary for 1 July 1916,

> We were delayed taking off as the mechanic had over filled with oil, but we were off by 7.20am. and over the lines by Zero Hour 7.30am. It was an awful sight to see our men lying out in lines opposite Beaumont Hamel, either dead or wounded. Only in two places did I see any of our troops reach the German trenches, and only a handful at each. I got a bullet into my buttock whilst we were at 2,000ft over Beaumont Hamel, the bullet having gone through our petrol tank first, there was no future in staying out, so we returned. I went to the Squadron Office and gave a verbal report to Brock who disbelieved me at the time. (Events subsequently proved me right). I walked up to my hut in the woods and the R.A.M.C. Orderly came and patched me up, having pulled bits of horse hair and petrol tank out of the hole.

> After about a couple of hours the ambulance arrived and took me to Gizaucourt. Tucker, the other Contact Patrol Observer, was also wounded by a bullet that went through the fleshy part of both legs, thus acquiring four holes from one bullet. The hospital very quickly filled up to overflowing and I spent an unpleasant night on a stretcher on the floor.[12]

It is hardly surprising that Packe, with an uncomfortable though not serious wound, was a low priority for treatment, as he waited to have the bullet extracted. When he was attended to, he was taken for an X-ray, the image showing the location of the projectile.

The battle in the air continued to rage as July passed by. Cooperation between ground troops and aircraft was in its infancy during the Battle of the Somme, but none the less there were flashes of the potential, which existed if the two arms could be made to work in unison. Cecil Lewis, a pilot with No. 56 Squadron RFC, recorded in his logbook for 16 July 1916,

> Our fellows almost entirely occupy High Wood. Called for flares with Klaxon. Splendid co-operation! We came lower, and Hun gave away his position by opening machine-gun fire on us. Located parties of bombers from Pozières to High Wood. Hun put up Very lights and turned machine-guns on us again. We cleared up the whole position. Job earned congratulations of General, Colonel and Major.[13]

Aircraft had demonstrated their value in terms of observation and reconnaissance right from the outset of the war, but the Battle of the Somme witnessed the first concerted effort in the history of warfare to use an air arm directly in tactical support of a ground offensive. Sir Hugh Trenchard, commander of the RFC, believed that its role was entirely subordinate to the needs of the ground forces. He knew that it would be costly in terms of aircraft and aircrew lives (and some 400 were to be lost over the Somme) but he intended to dominate the skies that summer through aggressive patrolling, thereby denying the German air force the opportunity to use its own machines to interfere with the advance through aerial observation. Less glamorous than the single seat fighters, but probably of greater importance to the overall campaign were the two seat reconnaissance aircraft. They provided information to the artillery as to German gun positions and troop movements. The work of spotting and photographing German positions was extremely hazardous, and this was not solely due to the fact that observation aircraft were invariably slower than the enemy fighters.

Another pairing from No. 3 Squadron were Lieutenant Howard O. Long and Captain Alfred J. Evans. They were again on a reconnaissance flight, likewise on 16 July 1916 when it appears their Morane Parasol was hit by fire from the ground, an ever-present danger over the Somme battlefield. As Evans testified, the machine was hit in either the magneto or the petrol tank, which caused the engine to give out 10 miles over the German lines north-east of Bapaume. Later in the war, great emphasis would be placed on ensuring that flying crews took nothing into the air with them that might help the enemy:

Above left: Air Mechanic James McCudden, who arrived in France in 1914 with No 3 Squadron RFC. (Author's Collection)

Above right: Second Lieutenant Gilbert Mapplebeck, one of the pioneers of ground attack tactics in 1914, was awarded a DSO for his daring bombing raid on a German ammunition column. (Author's Collection)

Below: A German convoy destroyed by Mapplebeck, September 1914. (Author's Collection)

Above: Royal Navy Parseval HM *Airship No 4*, which served on patrol work in 1914. It was this vessel, commanded by Lieutenant John Fletcher, which was fired upon by British Territorial troops. (Library of Congress)

Left: An artist's impression of the Cuxhaven Raid, Christmas Day 1914. (Library of Congress)

Lieutenant Commander John Cyril Porte. He was posted to Felixstowe in September 1915 as commander of the Experimental Flying Wing. He modified the hull of the larger Curtiss H-12 flying boat, creating the Felixstowe F.2, which was greatly superior to the original Curtiss boat. The Felixstowes were mainly used on long-range patrols, to look for the High Seas Fleet or submarines of the Imperial German Navy. (Library of Congress)

An F5L Felixstowe Flying Boat, with another in the distance. This was one of the Felixstowe F series of flying boats developed by John Cyril Porte at the Seaplane Experimental Station, Felixstowe, in 1918. (Library of Congress)

Above: The aircraft carrier HMS *Furious*. The forward turret was removed during construction and replaced with a hangar and flight deck. In 1918 the rear turret would also be removed. (Library of Congress)

Left: Flight Commander Reginald Bone RNAS, who was station commander at Detling. In March 1916 flying from RNAS Westgate he forced down the first German raider of the war, a two-seater seaplane. (Library of Congress)

A recruiting advertisement lists the various trades required by the RFC. (Author's Collection)

Aircraftsman 2nd Class Harold W. Downes served with 10 Group Headquarters in South Western England in June 1918. He was an Aero Rigger by trade. (Author's Collection)

Above: The Night Hawks – Lieutenant James Galletly Morton, Royal Scots attached RAF, seated front row fifth from left. The location is likely to be No 44 Training Depot Station, Oxford, in 1918. (Author's Collection)

Below left: Three RFC mechanics at Niagara Falls, 1917, including Corporal Coppler and Aircraftsman 1st Class Smith. They were based at the RFC training centre at Toronto. (Author's Collection)

Below right: Captain Geoffrey H. Bonnell served with No 32 Squadron RFC from July to December 1916, flying the DH2. He was an American of Canadian descent, who began the war as a Gunner in the Canadian Field Artillery. (Library of Congress)

Right: A poster calling for women to join the WRAF, 1918. (Author's Collection)

Below: Women of the WRAF at work on an airframe of an Avro 504. (RAF Museum/Public Domain)

Left: Sub-Lieutenant Reginald 'Rex' Warneford was a Royal Naval Air Service officer whose daring attack on the German airship LZ37, in June 1915, earned him the Victoria Cross. (Library of Congress)

Below: BE2b serial number 487 of No 4 Squadron RFC, in German hands. It was reported missing on 11 March 1915. (Library of Congress)

Right: The grave of Captain Robert Pike of No 5 Squadron RFC, buried by German forces in August 1915. His grave was later lost. (Author's Collection)

Below: Lieutenant L.R. Heywood and Second Lieutenant D.B. Gayford of No 20 Squadron RFC, after being forced down in combat on 9 March 1916 whilst flying in FE2b 6356, escorting a reconnaissance patrol near Annapes. Steam was seen to be escaping from the engine after the radiator was holed by a bullet, and the machine landed at Ligny. Both officers escaped from captivity later in the war. (Author's Collection)

Above left: Second Lieutenant H.L.C. Aked, reported missing on 21 May 1916. He was the observer aboard a No 20 Squadron FE2b number 5206, shot down by Leutnant Wilhelm Frankl. Aked and his pilot Captain C.E.H. James subsequently posed with the German officer in front of their downed machine. (Author's Collection)

Above right: The German ace Leutnant Wilhelm Frankl, an early exponent of the Fokker *Eindecker.* (Library of Congress)

Left: Lieutenant Edward Packe (seen here earlier as a private soldier) flew with No 15 Squadron RFC over the battlefield at Beaumont Hamel on 1 July 1916. His reports of the unfolding disaster there were initially disbelieved. (Courtesy of Jo Edkins)

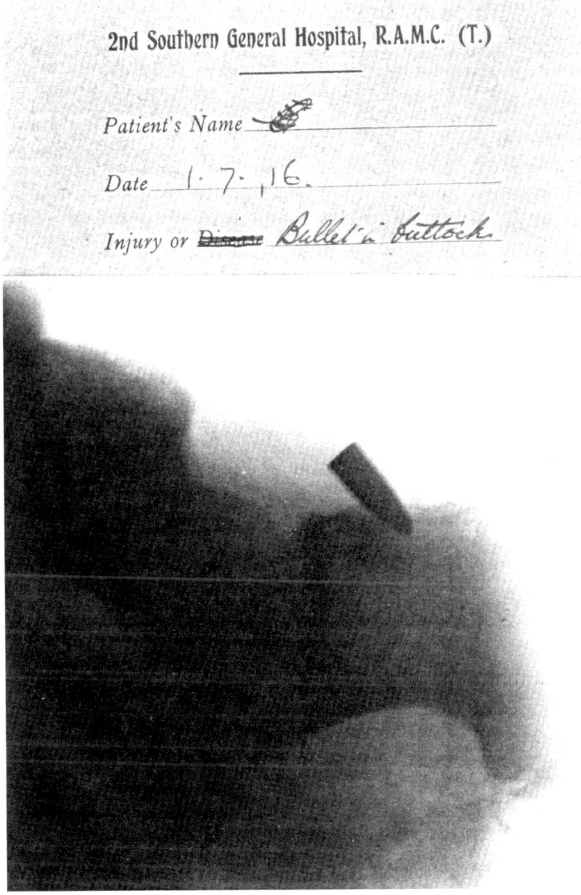

Right: An X-Ray photograph of Packe's buttock, showing the embedded bullet, which he received on 1 July 1916 over Beaumont Hamel. (Courtesy of Jo Edkins)

Below: Boelcke climbs from his Fokker *Eindecker* after returning from a sortie on the Somme front, 1916. (Author's Collection)

Above: A German aviator, one of a two-man reconnaissance crew, receiving orders. (Library of Congress)

Below: The view through the tail struts of a De Havilland DH2 'pusher' over the Somme battlefield in September 1916. The white puffs are exploding anti-aircraft shells. (Author's Collection)

Right: Flight Lieutenant J.C.P. Wood, one of the original pilots of the famous 'Naval 8' Squadron, RNAS at Dunkirk in 1916. (Library of Congress)

Below: Wreckage of a British aircraft shot down on 4 March 1917. (Author's Collection)

Above left: Air Mechanic 2nd Class Frank A.Hadlow was an Aerial Gunner aboard an FE2b, serial number 4954, of No 11 Squadron RFC. He was shot down during a defensive patrol west of Boyelles, on 1 April 1917, and taken as a POW to Lens, then on to Dulmen. (Author's Collection)

Above right: Lieutenant William Norman Hamilton (left) at Bad Colberg prisoner of war camp. He was shot down on 29 April 1917. (Author's Collection)

Left: Adolphus, the mascot of Captain Maurice Le Blanc Smith RFC. He was given the toy by a girlfriend and carried it throughout the war. (Author's Collection)

Above: A Royal Air Force Caquot kite balloon about to ascend with air mechanics holding the ropes, Gosnay, France, 2 May 1918. (Library of Congress)

Right: Lieutenant Curtis Matthew De Rochie, a Canadian pilot with No 27 Squadron RFC, flying Spads. He was shot down and killed over Ostende on 14 July 1917. He had been with the squadron only since the beginning of June. (Courtesy of Patrick Gariepy)

Above: De Haviland DH4 B2098 was a presentation aircraft, named Jamnagar No 2. This and two others were presented by Indian Maharajah Prince Ranjitsinghi in 1917. The aircraft was received at a Reception Park on 24 February 1918. (Author's Collection)

Below: RFC air mechanics load Lewis Gun magazines with .303 rounds at an airfield in France. The magazine for the aircraft-mounted Lewis was twice the size of the forty-seven round infantry version, so it needed to be changed less often. (Library of Congress)

Above: Bristol Fighter A7231 was shot down by *Jastu* 5, and landed intact behind enemy lines on 17 October 1917. There are numerous photos of it in subsequent German markings, but this rare image shows curious German troops examining the aircraft directly after it landed, and before the Lewis Gun was removed. (Author's Collection)

Below: Four RFC pilots consult a map at an airfield in France. Note the variety of flying clothing. (Library of Congress)

Above: The pilot and observer of a Royal Aircraft Factory RE8 (serial number B5106) of No 59 Squadron RAF receiving instructions from Major Charles Joseph Mackay before taking off from the Vert-Galland Aerodrome, France, 15 May 1918. The observer's Lewis Gun is on a Scarff ring. (Library of Congress)

Left: Leading Mechanic Thomas Weatherald RNAS was an Aeroplane Rigger, and served with Naval 11 Squadron in France from February 1918. The squadron was based near Dunkirk and operated DH4 and DH9 bombers against U-boat bases on the Belgian coast. (Author's Collection)

Above left: Air Mechanic 2nd Class James T. Caiger, from Manchester. A motor fitter before the war, he served from 1917 with the Royal Flying Corps Engine Repair Shops, his trade being Engine Fitter. (Author's Collection)

Above right: Air Mechanic 1st Class Harry Holyoake, a Motor Transport Driver at Number 3 Army Aircraft Park. He was a chauffeur from Leeds in civil life. He was awarded the Meritorious Service Medal at the end of the war. (Author's Collection)

Right: Corporal Bill Sainsbury of No 48 Squadron RAF was shot down near Villers Bretoneux in May 1918. The pilot suffered fatal injuries and Sainsbury was wounded. He spent the remainder of the war in a prison camp, where this photo was taken. (Author's Collection)

Above: The enormous Handley Page 0400 dwarfs the workmen putting on the final touches, 1918. (Library of Congress)

Below left: Paul Baumer, a German ace with 43 confirmed kills, nicknamed 'The Iron Eagle'. His country's ninth highest scoring pilot, he was awarded the Pour Le Merite, Germany's greatest honour. He was one of the few pilots of either side whose life was saved by a parachute, after he was shot down in September 1918. (Author's Collection)

Below right: Private 2nd Class Thomas Arthur Hetherington. He enlisted in the RAF in August 1918 and was posted to 212 Training Depot Station, Vendome, France. His trade was Motorcyclist. (Author's Collection)

Above: HMS *Ark Royal*, a seaplane carrier in the Dardanelles. She was originally laid down as a merchantman but was purchased by the Royal Navy whilst on the stocks at Blyth in 1914, and converted. (Library of Congress)

Below: Commander Charles Rumney Samson and some of his officers. (Author's Collection)

Left: Sergeant Mechanic Ronald C.Chapman RAF was ex-RNAS. He had served at HMS *Queen* II with seaplanes on Malta since 1916; he continued to do so into the summer of 1918, being promoted to Observer in July. He was awarded the Distinguished Flying Medal. (Author's Collection)

Below: The stern of HMS *Ben-My-Chree*, at Mudros. Note the aircraft in the hangar. (Public Domain)

Above: The presentation of the DCM to Air Mechanic First Class Samuel Hall, 31 Wing Royal Flying Corps, at an aerodrome in Mesopotamia. The award was for maintaining radio communication with an aircraft whilst he was under enemy fire. (Courtesy of Stuart Brown)

Right: As part of the Aegean operations the RNAS maintained Balloon Base No 4, at Corfu. Air Mechanic 2nd Class Raymond George Hopkins was serving there in 1918, as an Airship Rigger. (Author's Collection)

Above: British and French troops inspect the remains of a German two-seater brought down on the Macedonian front, 1917. (Library of Congress)

Below: An RAF concert party c1918. It was in a similar troupe that Jack Warner ('Dixon of Dock Green') began his acting career. (Author's Collection)

I found myself hanging upside down by my belt. I was a bit shaken but unhurt, and got out quickly. Long was staggering about in a very dazed condition near the machine, and the Germans were about 50 yards away. I got a matchbox from him and crawled under the machine again, but found, firstly, that I could not reach the petrol tap, and in spite of the machine being upside down, there was no petrol dripping anywhere; and, secondly, that Long in his dazed condition had handed me a box without any matches in it. The Germans were now about 25 yards off, and I thought of trying to set the thing on fire with the Lewis gun and tracer bullets, but I could not find the gun. I think Long must have thrown it overboard as we came down. We were then surrounded by soldiers – they were a filthy crowd, but showed no signs of unpleasantness. An officer, whose face I disliked, came up, and, saluting very correctly, asked me to hand over all my papers and maps. Rather than be searched, I turned out my own and Long's pockets for him. In doing so, I found to my horror that I had my diary on me! Why, I can't think, as I was always most careful to go up without any paper of importance, and particularly without my diary. However, I managed to keep it from the Germans, and got rid of it about an hour later without being detected. We walked with the German officer to the Gondecourt road, and I was glad to see as we went away, that the machine seemed thoroughly smashed up. The propeller was smashed and nose plate obviously bent badly; one wing and the under carriage were crumpled

> up. The elevator was broken, and it looked as if something had gone in the fuselage, but I could not be certain of that. Long was thoroughly shaken, and walked and talked like a drunken man. He kept on asking questions, which he reiterated in the most maddening way – poor chap – but to be asked every two minutes if you had been captured, when you are surrounded by a crowd of beastly Huns! I own I was feeling pretty irritable at the time, and perhaps a bit shaken.[14]

Captain Robert Saundby meanwhile served with Major Lanoe Hawker's famous No. 24 Squadron, RFC, which so dominated the Somme battlefield that summer. Saundby was based at Bertangles, behind the Somme front, and remembered that life at an airfield was for the most part peaceful:

> It was a good aerodrome: just across the railway, which runs in a cutting behind the sheds, there lived a cheery squadron of F.E. 2b's. No. 11. Here ... there [was] nothing to suggest war, except a distant muttering and grumbling of guns ... [When] the last to come home of the patrol, a little delayed by one of the hundred and one causes that might delay him, turns up at last, however [an] almost unconscious relief is felt at the sight of the overdue pilot dropping into the aerodrome ... The quiet village, quiet except when the squadron billeted there was celebrating some occasion in the evening, [stood] in the background.[15]

By now the British were clearly gaining the advantage over the Fokker *Eindecker* monoplane, which had done such damage the previous year. Saundby remembered a particular characteristic of this aircraft:

> Side-slipping was a favourite trick of the Fokker when caught, and they could lose height very quickly by this method. The Fokker was not very strong however, and occasionally they broke up when trying to 'stunt' to get away from attack ... Apropos the liability of the Fokker to break up, I know an interesting case in point which occurred in the squadron in which I was serving at the time. Captain ______ was leading a patrol of two D.H.2's and had been asked to keep an eye on a B.E.2C that was out on photography. He found he had climbed rather too high to be able to watch the B.E. sufficiently closely, and decided to lose a couple of thousand feet. He did so and flattened out a few hundred up over the B.E.2C, which was then about 8,000 feet. He thought no more about the matter until, on arriving home, the B.E.2C squadron telephoned and warmly thanked him for saving the Photographic B.E.2C from a Fokker, which, they said, he had brought down and crashed near. On investigation it appeared that the Fokker had been climbing up under the B.E.2C to attack it, had seen the Scout patrol diving on him, and spun down and away so violently as to break up in the air and finally crash.[16]

Saundby comments on the fact that during this period of the war, before the Albatros began to appear in German squadrons in significant numbers later that autumn, most enemy fighter pilots were reluctant to cross the front and fight over allied territory. The only such pilot willing to do so regularly was Oswald Boelcke, of whom Saundby says:

> [He], however, was one of the few Huns in those days who did come over our lines. He was a brave man, and commanded more admiration in the Flying Corps in his day, than, I venture to think, any other German Pilot since the war began.

Boelcke for his part wrote of a number of encounters with the pilots of the RFC in July 1916, from which his tally of 'kills' might have been higher were it not for the unreliability of his armament:

> I made good use of my chance to again attack the English at D. I liked it so well, I kept postponing my return to S. One evening I flew a Halberstadt biplane; this was the first appearance of these machines at the front. As it is somewhat similar to an English B.-E., I succeeded in completely fooling an Englishman. I got to within fifty meters of him and fired a number of shots at him. But as I was flying quite rapidly, and was not as familiar with the new machine as with the Fokker, I did not succeed in hitting him right away. I passed beneath him, and he turned and started to descend. I followed him, but

> my cartridge belt jammed and I could not fire. I turned away, and before I had repaired the damage he was gone. The next day I had two more opportunities to attack Englishmen. The first time, it was a squadron of six Vickers' machines. I started as they were over L., and the other Fokkers from D. went with me. As I had the fastest machine, I was first to reach the enemy. I picked out one and shot at him, with good results; his motor (behind the pilot) puffed out a great quantity of yellow smoke. I thought he would fall any moment, but he escaped by gliding behind his own line. According to the report of our infantry, he was seen to land two kilometers behind the front. I could not finish him entirely, because my left gun had run out of ammunition, and the right one had jammed. In the meantime, the other Fokkers had reached the English. I saw one 160-horsepower machine (Mulzer, pilot) attack an Englishman in fine style, but as the Englishman soon received aid, I had to come to Mulzer's rescue. So I drove the one away from Mulzer; my enemy did not know I was unable to fire at him. Mulzer saw and recognized me, and again attacked briskly. To my regret, he had only the same success I had had a while before, and as Mulzer turned to go home, I did likewise. In the afternoon, I again had a chance at an Englishman, but he escaped in the clouds.[17]

The Battle of the Somme has claim to a special place in the history of the German air force. It became the high school of aviation tactics and skills, it had a crucial influence on both its organisational and technical developments, and shaped the training provided to flight crews until the war ended. Furthermore, these developments came to the fore at the same time as many as virulent attacks were being made in Germany by alleged experts concerning the supposed failures of German flyers before and at the beginning of the battle. These claims even reached the proceedings of the Reichstag in Berlin, and astoundingly, German pilots who were were sorely needed in this period at the front had to leave their units to give evidence there. They underwent their thankless task with good will, and were able to refute the validity of these claims, largely because the evidence was obtained from records studied from the safety of a chair at a desk, and from which the weight of personal experience gained in the pilot or observer's seat was absent. Among the students of Boelcke in 1916 was a young Manfred von Richthofen, later to become famous in his own right (indeed even more famous than his mentor). He wrote of his experiences in aerial combat that summer:

> During my whole life I have not found a happier hunting ground than in the course of the Somme Battle. In the morning, as soon as I had got up, the first Englishmen arrived, and the last did not disappear until long after sunset. Boelcke once said that this was the El Dorado of the flying men. There was a time when, within two months, Boelcke's bag of machines increased from twenty to forty. We beginners had not at that time the experience of our master and we were quite satisfied when we did not get a hiding. It was an exciting period. Every time

> we went up we had a fight. Frequently we fought really big battles in the air. There were sometimes from forty to sixty English machines, but unfortunately the Germans were often in the minority. With them quality was more important than quantity.
>
> Still the Englishman is a smart fellow. That we must allow. Sometimes the English came down to a very low altitude and visited Boelcke in his quarters, upon which they threw their bombs. They absolutely challenged us to battle and never refused fighting. We had a delightful time with our chasing squadron. The spirit of our leader animated all his pupils. We trusted him blindly. There was no possibility that one of us would be left behind. Such a thought was incomprehensible to us. Animated by that spirit we gaily diminished the number of our enemies.[18]

If the German fighter pilots were reluctant to cross the lines, for two-seater reconnaissance aircraft and their crews, it was part and parcel of their daily duties. The demand for accurate information about the movements of the enemy grew ever greater, and both sides continued to pay the price of the 'eye in the sky'. Whilst the single seater pilots such as Boelcke and von Richthofen attracted most of the fame and glory, steady, monotonous but just as dangerous work was done by the crews of two-seater Pfalz aircraft on photo reconnaissance work. The commander of Bavarian Artillery Flieger Abteilung 102, Hauptmann Schwink, recounted an incident, which occurred over the French lines on 29 July 1916:

Two of us were to record the enemy positions south of the Somme in photographs. Cherdron, for whom the machine gun was closer to the heart than was the camera, wanted to provide cover for his friends. It was a beautiful morning as the three headed out. The enemy, who likes to sleep late, appeared not to be present, and Cherdron's cover vouched for complete safety. The peace, however, was deceptive. When the machines flew over the enemy, up they came. Cherdron took on the first and was pushed by the air battle far from the others. Even as he disappeared from the view of the neighbouring planes, three other single seaters attacked. In a frantic dive the leader of the force tried to escape. Cherdron had received a bullet to the heart, and Sergeant Mielcareck was shot twice in the chest and in the leg. The plane crashed. The others could not see Cherdron's fight. They had to carry out their orders and fulfilled their mission despite several battles.

As I stood at the aerodrome, and saw only two come back, my heart skipped a beat. At first we were not afraid. For when our Cherdron was hunting, it often got late. An hour passed; then another; concern was growing and we began to make inquiries in the hope that Cherdron had made an emergency landing somewhere. But no one knew anything about him. It was not until late in the evening that we received notice from an artillery commander, who said that Cherdron's aeroplane had been hit in combat, Cherdron was dead, [and] the aircraft's pilot Mielcareck, who was severely wounded, had destroyed the machine.

That evening it was quiet in our quarters. Volunteer teams led by Cherdron's friends brought the dead comrades in from the artillery fire; the brave, wounded pilot was taken to a field hospital, where he died after twelve hours. We carried the comrades to the church of Ham and buried them in the cemetery. It was the worst path we had so far taken. The Grim Reaper had announced his presence, and so the fittest and most notable were now torn from our midst; on the way home, we promised all of us that at least the enemy should not notice the gap that had arisen in our little group. I knew my flyers. Their young hearts, which had become so soft at the grave, regained their strength within the hour. Their courage was unbroken, they had already flown a great deal, and now they flew even more so as to avenge the dead. In the shortest time our whole front was re-photographed. So began the detailed work of directing artillery fire on to observed targets and the constant monitoring of the front.

... Despite the considerable effort and dangers to which without exception all were subjected, towards the end of the battle my little group was still faithfully together. We were reinforced and the new ones which came had to pass a variety of tests, both in and out of service, until they were deemed to be the equivalent of the 'ancients'. The Battle of the Somme had demanded the extreme use of force. It had made my young airmen into veterans.[19]

As an insight into the fierce comradeship that grew up among a squadron of pilots, this account is particularly powerful. The pilot mentioned in the above incident, Unteroffizier Max Stanislaus Mielcareck died of wounds at Pargny on 30 July 1916, whilst the observer Leutnant Phillip Cherdron as stated was killed in the action. He was a holder of the Iron Cross First and Second Class and the Bavarian MVO, and now lies buried in the cemetery at Ludwigshafen, in central Germany; it would appear that his family were able to arrange for the repatriation of his body.

The technique of aerial bombing in the RFC had advanced but little since Mapplebeck's attack on a convoy in 1914. P.S. Jackson-Taylor, an F.E.2b observer with No. 16 Squadron recounted,

> Usually two or four 20lb bombs were carried on each patrol and dropped whenever and wherever the pilot wished. I do not remember any form of standard bomb sighting being used. Consequently the bombing was of a very elementary character and the absence of individual knowledge of the principles of Bomb Dropping made the process of pulling the release toggle a delightful game of chance. I shall never forget peering over the side to watch the effects of a salvo of two bombs on the German trenches at Martinpuich [and] my consternation on seeing the bombs fall and burst quite half a mile away to the west in front of our own front line.[20]

Just north of the Somme battlefield, No. 18 Squadron were also engaged on this work, likewise equipped with F.E.2b aircraft.

In these machines, the engine was mounted at the back, the pilot in front of it, with the observer/gunner in the forward compartment, armed with a forward-facing Lewis machine-gun, and one mounted on the upper wing. To fire this weapon the observer stood up, his knees level with the sides of the cockpit, no seatbelt to hold him in, and only his grip on the gun standing between him and eternity, should the pilot dive or swoop suddenly. It must have been a terrifying experience if, and when, it happened. Among their crews was Captain Elgie Jefferson, an officer of the King's Liverpool Regiment, attached to the RFC, and serving now as an observer. In one hair raising incident on 30 August 1916, Jefferson who was in the forward gunner's compartment of an F.E.2b, clung on helplessly as the machine drifted out of control after it was attacked over enemy lines, and the pilot was wounded. Fortunately the pilot recovered consciousness before the machine struck the ground, and he was able to bring it down in a controlled crash landing at a British aerodrome. Not surprisingly, Jefferson's injuries were not confined to physical bruising. His medical notes mention 'nerve shock', and whilst on convalescent leave after the incident he wrote to his superiors:

> I have the honour to apply for 3 weeks leave of absence from my squadron in the field, on medical grounds. I was given special leave which expires on the 19th [September] for medical reasons. My nerves are very strained and I feel very run down and do not feel fit enough to carry out my work as an observer, for the present… [21]

Aged just 20, Jefferson none the less recovered his nerve, and in a subsequent letter to the authorities expressed his wish to return to flying duties. He later qualified as a pilot. With life expectancy for aircrew on the Western Front now measured in weeks, as well as a glamorous and dashing reputation, airmen often had a 'live for the moment' attitude. Jefferson was no exception to this rule, and the following year he was treated in hospital for gonorrhoea.

Never the less, by autumn 1916, bad weather and heavy cloud cover was rendering aerial observation increasingly difficult. Aircraft were either grounded altogether, or their view of the enemy lines was obscured. As a French intelligence officer noted, when information received from airmen was positive, in as much as they had seen something, this was useful. However when they stated that they had not seen anything, this was much less reliable for bodies of troops could easily be hidden in railway cuttings, woods or buildings. Unlike the French, who took an ad-hoc mission-by-mission approach, in the British service infantry observers were generally attached to RFC squadrons on a considerably longer-term basis, in fact for the duration of the war, which allowed for a greater degree of training. The offensive spirit in the RFC was also much more prevalent. As evidence of this we have the account of Alan Bott, a second lieutenant with a commission in the Royal Garrison Artillery, who flew as an observer with No. 70 Squadron RFC operating from Fienvillers in autumn 1916. Bott flew on patrol work over the Somme battlefield and wrote,

Punctually at five o'clock [am] the order, 'Start up!' passed down the long line of machines. The flight-commander's engine began a loud metallic roar, then softened as it was throttled down. The pilot waved his hand, the chocks were pulled from under the wheels, and the machine moved forward. The throttle was again opened full out as the bus raced into the wind until flying speed had been attained, when it skimmed gently from the ground. We followed, and carried out the rendezvous at 3,000 feet.

The morning light increased every minute, and the grey of the sky was merging into blue. The faint, hovering ground-mist was not sufficient to screen our landmarks. The country below was a shadowy patchwork of coloured pieces. The woods, fantastic shapes of dark green, stood out strongly from the mosaic of brown and green fields. The pattern was divided and subdivided by the straight, poplar-bordered roads peculiar to France.

We passed on to the dirty strip of wilderness which is the actual front. The battered villages and disorderly ruins looked like hieroglyphics traced on wet sand. A sea of smoke rolled over the ground for miles. It was a by-product of one of the most terrific bombardments in the history of trench warfare. Through it hundreds of gun-flashes twinkled, like the lights of a Chinese garden.

Having reached a height of 12,000 feet, we crossed the trenches south of Bapaume. As the danger that stray bullets might fall on friends no longer existed, pilots and observers fired a few rounds into space to make sure their guns were behaving properly.[22]

The squadron operated Sopwith 1½ Strutters, two-seater aircraft with a forward-facing Vickers gun operated by the pilot, and a Lewis gun operated by an observer in the rear cockpit. Bott soon became involved in a dogfight, and the fickle nature of both aircraft and armament are made clear:

> I looked down and saw eight machines with black Maltese crosses on their planes, about three thousand feet below. They had clipped wings of a peculiar whiteness, and they were ranged one above the other, like the rungs of a Venetian blind. A cluster of small scouts swooped down from Heaven-knows-what height and hovered above us; but C. evidently did not see them, for he dived steeply on the Huns underneath, accompanied by the two machines nearest him. The other group of enemies then dived on us.
>
> I looked up and saw a narrow biplane, apparently a Roland, rushing towards our bus. My pilot turned vertically and then side-slipped to disconcert the Boche's aim. The black –crossed craft swept over at a distance of less than a hundred yards. I raised my gun-mounting, sighted, and pressed the trigger. Three shots rattled off – and my Lewis gun ceased fire.
>
> Intensely annoyed at being cheated out of such a splendid target, I applied immediate action, pulled back the cocking-handle and pressed the trigger again.

Nothing happened. After one more immediate action test, I examined the gun and found that an incoming cartridge and an empty case were jambed together in the breech. To remedy the stoppage, I had to remove spade-grip and body-cover. As I did this, I heard an ominous ta-ta-ta-ta-ta from the returning German scout. My pilot cart-wheeled round and made for the Hun, his gun spitting continuously through the propeller. The two machines raced at each other until less than fifty yards separated them. Then the Boche swayed, turned aside, and put his nose down. We dropped after him, with our front machine-gun still speaking. The Roland's glide merged into a dive, and we imitated him. Suddenly a streak of flame came from his petrol tank, and the next second he was rushing earthwards, with two streamers of smoke trailing behind.

I was unable to see the end of this vertical dive, for two more single-seaters were upon us. They plugged away while I remedied the stoppage, and several bullets ventilated the fuselage quite close to my cockpit. When my gun was itself again, I changed the drum of ammunition, and hastened to fire at the nearest Hun. He was evidently unprepared, for he turned and moved across our tail. As he did so, I raked his bus from stem to stern. I looked at him hopefully, for the range was very short, and I expected to see him drop towards the ground at several miles a minute. He sailed on serenely. This is an annoying habit of enemy machines when one is sure that, by the rules of the game, they ought to be

> destroyed. The machine in question was probably hit, however, for it did not return, and I saw it begin a glide as though the pilot meant to land. We switched our attention to the remaining Hun, but this one was not anxious to fight alone. He dived a few hundred feet, with tail well up, looking for all the world like a trout when it drops back into water. Afterwards he flattened out and went east.[23]

German pilot Oswald Boelcke was now notching up an impressive tally of kills flying on the Somme at this time, as he wrote in a letter to his parents:

> On September 27th [1916] I met seven English machines, near B. I had started on a patrol flight with four of my men, and we saw a squadron I first thought was German. When we met southwest of B., I saw they were enemy 'planes. We were lower and I changed my course. The Englishmen passed us, flew over to us, flew around our kite-balloon and then set out for their own front. However, in the meantime, we had reached their height and cut off their retreat. I gave the signal to attack, and a general battle started. I attacked one; got too close; ducked under him and, turning, saw an Englishman fall like a plummet.
>
> As there were enough others left I picked out a new one. He tried to escape, but I followed him. I fired round after round into him. His stamina surprised me. I felt he should have fallen long ago, but he kept going in the

same circle. Finally, it got too much for me. I knew he was dead long ago, and by some freak, or due to elastic controls, he did not change his course. I flew quite close to him and saw the pilot lying dead, half out of his seat. To know later which was the 'plane I had shot down (for eventually he must fall), I noted the number – 7495. Then I left him and attacked the next one. He escaped, but I left my mark on him. As I passed close under him I saw a great hole I had made in his fuselage. He will probably not forget this day. I had to work like a Trojan. Number 30 was very simple, I surprised a scout above our front – we call these scouts '*Häschen*' (rabbits) – fired at him; he tilted, and disappeared. The fall of Number 31 was a wonderful sight. We, five men and myself, were amusing ourselves attacking every French or English machine we saw, and firing our guns to test them. This did not please our opponents at all. Suddenly, far below me, I saw one fellow circling about, and I went after him. At close range I fired at him, aiming steadily. He made things easy for me, flying a straight course. I stayed twenty or thirty meters behind him and pounded him till he exploded with a great yellow flare. We cannot call this a fight, because I surprised my opponent. Everything goes well with me; healthy, good food, good quarters, good companions, and plenty to do.[24]

Boelcke's victory number thirty-one was a Nieuport Scout, which crashed near Morval. The aircraft that a few days previously had flown on like a ghost ship, despite having a dead pilot, was a Martinsyde G.100 of No. 27 Squadron, RFC. As Boelcke had predicted it crashed later on 27 September 1916 behind enemy lines, the pilot Second Lieutenant Stephen Dendrino being buried at Beurains Road Cemetery.

That same month an experienced British pilot returned to the fray after being wounded the previous year. He was Second Lieutenant Frank Courtney, posted to No. 20 Squadron (operating F.E.2 aircraft), another British squadron that was to gain the 'Somme' battle honour. Courtney had interesting observations to make both on the relative merits of British and German aircraft and of British versus German tactics. He makes the point in his memoirs that almost all the air fighting on the Somme took place over German-held territory because this was a deliberate choice by the Germans. Courtney points out that the great Boelcke (who he also describes as the only German airman truly respected in the RFC) was the only enemy pilot prepared to cross the British lines, and yet even he was not ashamed to proclaim the uninspiring slogan of the German air service 'Let the customer come to us.' Courtney further adds that this situation, and the aggressive attitude of the RFC of which he was so proud, was all the more remarkable when one considers the great inferiority in machinery, which the British had previously suffered. Now however the RFC was gaining the upper hand against the German Fokker *Eindecker.* Courtney continues,

> … we did have a number of planes, such as the F.E.s to which I was now assigned, that could at least fight back when they were attacked, even though they were

much too slow and unwieldy to take the offensive. With them we carried out our so-called fighter patrols by cruising around over hostile territory with chips on our shoulders, defying the enemy to attack us. When they did, they had all the advantages of the initiative, but they did not always escape lightly, and occasionally they fared very badly ... The F.E.2 was a remarkable airplane – which is not intended as a compliment, because the most remarkable facts about it were that it was ever called a 'fighter' and that it was retained in service for so long and in such numbers. It was a ponderous, 2 seat pusher biplane of nearly 50 foot span, as compared to the 28 foot monoplane span of the Fokker. Its great size and rocklike stability made it as manoeuvrable as a cathedral, and it was impossible to dive it: at anything much over a hundred miles an hour with nose down, the elevator control would overcome the pilot and the stick would push itself hard back into his lap whilst the plane levelled off. I had devised a trick method of diving it by first hauling it up into a stall and then holding it down when it fell off into a dive, but enemy fighters were not disposed to wait around while I performed this ceremony. It had twenty-eight exposed struts and booms for its wing and tail structures (and eleven more for the landing gear), with endless fathoms of connecting wires. With these built-in head winds, no amount of power could give it any useful speed, so when our F.E.2d's acquired the 250 hp Rolls Royce engine, as compared with the 120hp of the original F.E2b, the increase in speed was

> almost negligible. The extra power did, however, give us a generous improvement in climb – and we needed it.
>
> Fighting on the F.E2 was like no other kind of fighting. The gunner's field of fire was an entire, unobstructed hemisphere of air space ahead, whilst the sometimes painful stability of the plane gave him a solidly steady platform to work from. On the other hand, anywhere below and behind the plane – and that was a lot of space – an enemy was completely safe from the F.E.'s gun, and the F.E. control was much too sluggish to evade attack from the rear. So a single F.E. could be sunk in short order by a fast and nimble enemy with the ability to get quickly behind it. This fact fooled the Fokkers for a long time into the belief that the F.E. was naturally easy meat. But a formation of F.E.s was a very nasty unit to attack. Our procedure, when attacked, was to break formation and swerve off in all directions, milling around and trying to keep as close together as reasonably possible. The Fokkers didn't like this at all, because an F.E. was in danger only when lined up squarely with a Fokker's fixed gun, whereas a Fokker was in danger any time it got at all in front of an F.E. and with several F.E.s weaving closely around, there was almost no time when a Fokker might not find itself heading the wrong way under the gun of at least one F.E.[25]

In order to increase the bomb load it was sometimes the practice to fly without an observer in two-seater machines. Second Lieutenant Gerald Featherstone Knight was an officer in the Devonshire Regiment who had been seconded to the RFC. Whilst serving with No. 12 Squadron, flying B.E.2c No. 2502, Knight took part in a bombing raid against Douai aerodrome on 9 November 1916. Flying without an observer he was particularly vulnerable when engine trouble caused him to lag behind his formation and its escorts. He was shot down behind German lines, near Mory:

> As my machine became more isolated I cast anxious glances about and was soon rewarded by seeing two wicked little enemy scouts waiting for an easy prey (at that time they did not usually attack a formation, but waited behind for the likes o' me). While one scout attracted my attention on the left and I was engaged in keeping him off by firing occasional bursts, a machine gun opened fire with a deafening clatter at point-blank range from behind. In an instant the surrounding air became full of innumerable tiny, brilliant flames, passing me at an incredible speed like minute streaks of lightning, each one giving forth a curious staccato whistling crack as it plunged through or beside the tormented machine, leaving in its wake a thin curling line of blue smoke. I was in the middle of a relentless storm of burning tracer bullets, vying one with the other for the honour of passing through the petrol tank, thereby converting my machine into a seething furnace. Having no observer to defend my tail I turned steeply to meet my new adversary. However, before completing the manoeuvre I received another deadly burst of fire,

which, though it somehow missed me, shot away several of my control wires. What happened next I cannot be sure, but the machine seemed to turn over, and my machine gun fell off with a crash. This took place at an altitude of six thousand feet. My next impression was that I seemed to be in the centre of a whirling vortex, around which all creation revolved at an extraordinary speed, and realised that my trusty steed was indulging in a particularly violent 'spinning nose dive'. A 'spin' at the best of times rather takes one's breath away, so, shutting the throttle, I endeavoured to come out of it in the usual way. To my surprise, the engine refused to slow down, or any of the controls to respond, except one, which only tended to make matters worse.

The one option left to the pilot was to switch the engine off, and trust to luck …

I vaguely thought there would be rather a splash when we arrived at our destination, but at eight hundred feet Providence came to the rescue. I heard the welcome cessation of the wild screaming hum of the strained wires. After switching on, the engine informed me with much spluttering that it was sorry that I should have to land on the wrong side, but it really had done its best. I had just managed to turn towards our trenches, when the scout pilot, seeing I did not land, at once followed me down and with its machine gun impressed on me that the sooner I landed the better. As I was then a long way over the lines, sinking fast towards the tree-tops, I had no alternative…[26]

Knight was furious at being captured, but the German soldiers who rushed up to the machine were surprised to be greeted with a cheery '*Gutten Morgen*'. This astonished them so much that they forgot to be rude, and mostly returned the compliment.

The Battle of the Somme ended on 18 November 1916. To some extent the aggressive attitude of the RFC forced the Germans to introduce new aircraft types in order just to maintain their advantage in equipment, and the arrival of new types of fighter, the Halberstadt and Albatros, on the Somme in September may be taken as evidence of this. Over the period of the Battle of the Somme, some 499 British pilots and observers were recorded as killed, wounded or missing in operations over the Western Front. Needless to say, the struggle to maintain air superiority over the battlefield, which was already proving costly to the allies, would become still more stern. None the less, morale was still extremely high among British flying personnel, as Sub-Lieutenant C.P.O. Bartlett remembered. He served at this time with No. 5 Naval Squadron at Coudekerque near Dunkirk, their aircraft attacked ports, harbours and shipping up the Belgian coast as far as the Dutch frontier, and targets included Ostend docks, wharves and submarine pens at Bruges, Zeebrugge Mole and shipping in the Zeebrugge-Bruges canal. Docks were particularly suitable for night attacks, as they showed up reasonably well even on a dark night. He remembered,

> Being a naval Wing we adopted naval terms; we saluted the 'Quarter Deck', attended 'Divisions' on Sundays,

> slept in 'cabins' and frequented the 'Ward Room' or 'Gun Room', 'went ashore' in the 'Liberty Boat', i.e. into Dunkirk in a Crossley Tender, the 'Lower Deck' were given 'make and mends' and detailed to 'port and starboard watches' by the 'master at Arms', and so on. It all worked out very well; we were an extremely happy station and right through all ranks there was a natural and unforced *esprit-de-corps* of a high standard.[27]

Christmas 1916 was almost ruined for him by a truculent old 'bus' aboard that he was due to return to the United Kingdom:

> What trick, I wondered, would old 8527 play on me this time – perhaps drop me in the 'drink' half way across the Channel! However, I took off and got to 500ft over the outskirts of Dunkirk when once again she cut dead. With no possibility of landing ahead, I turned back towards the aerodrome, dropping fast. As I had taken off into a brisk wind I dared not attempt a down-wind landing, especially as our Sopwiths were lined up in front of the hangars. At 60ft I attempted to turn into wind, but with no engine and insufficient height I could not get her round and at 40ft she fell out of my hands, hitting the ground on port wing and engine, all four longerons breaking just behind my back.
>
> 'Well', I thought, as I sat in the shambles, 'that's the end of you old girl, you've done your best to kill me, now you're dead and can trouble me no longer.' Finding I was still all in one piece and with nothing worse than

a few bruises and a black eye, I scrambled out of the debris. Jope Slade … and Norman Glaisby, who had witnessed my take-off and return, were running across the aerodrome to extricate my mangled remains, and would not believe me when I said I was quite all right and as steady as when I took off. A somewhat unfortunate Christmas Eve, and I turned in early with a thick head, making it an excuse to lie in next morning and so missing an inspection parade by Wing Captain C. L. Lambe who commanded the Group of RNAS units in the Dunkirk Command. I did not, however, miss our very hilarious Christmas Dinner in the evening which included many guests from other units. I still have, pasted in my diary, the dinner menu autographed by all present.[28]

Chapter Four

Western Front, 1917–1918

Throughout the winter months of 1916 to 1917 weather conditions interfered considerably with operational flying, especially during January and early February 1917. Northern France and Belgium experienced an intensely cold spell for weeks on end, with the thermometer reaching 10°C below 0°F (42°C of frost) on the night of 6 February 1917. On 3 February eight Sopwiths of No. 5 Naval Squadron had left at 4.45 am to raid Bruges docks. Only two pilots, Rouse and Nelles, reached the target, the others all suffering engine seizures due to the castor oil lubricant freezing to the consistency of tallow, and had to land at various points in the Belgian countryside. Fortunately, there was only one bad crash, with Flight Sub-Lieutenant J.C.P. Wood snapping the trunks of two young willows, the fuselage sliding between them and becoming a complete write-off. Wood was lucky to escape with nothing worse than cuts and bruises and a sprained ankle. C.P.O. Bartlett's memoirs give an insight into the daily routine of the squadron in bad weather:

> During these non-flying spells we found plenty to entertain us – sundry sports on the station, badminton in one of the Bessoneau hangars became quite popular,

> and we were always running into Dunkirk in the 'liberty boat' for drinks and occasional dinners.[1]

For a young airman, the air services had the advantage that, when not actually on flying duty, there was ample opportunity for interaction with civilians living near the aerodromes, which were usually located some distance behind the lines. Flight Sub-Lieutenant Eric Crundall of the famous Naval No. 8 Squadron and his fellow pilots made the most of the situation:

> 28 March 1917: After lunch I went to Lozinghem with Soar where he had got to know about a dozen French girls, all about seventeen years of age. He could not talk to them much because he did not know the French language very well so he wanted me to act as interpreter. All the girls congregated at Soar's billet where they were busy sewing most of the day. Soar's chief girlfriend was named Alexandra and was sixteen years of age. Soar introduced me to the girls as *Monsieur* Eric and said we would come back and see them in the evening.
>
> 30 March 1917: I went to Bethune in the afternoon with Arnold, Knight, Shields, Jenner-Parson and Simpson. This town is fairly close to the lines and occasionally it is shelled by the Germans. I was walking in the town with Jenner-Parson when two very good-looking girls waved to us from a kind of sports shop. Jenner waved back and the girls beckoned us to enter the shop. As soon as we entered they asked whether we would like some coffee.[2]

The two girls, Jacqueline and Fernande, invited them to call again next time they were in Bethune. That evening Crundall and a fellow officer, Bennetts, went to an estaminet where they met with another girl, Lydie who was 18 and very jolly. Lydie considered herself a cut above the other town girls as she was the only one who had visited Paris.

There was clearly a busy social life to be had if one wanted it. Captain Albert Ball, one of Britain's most famous of air fighters, however, was well-known among his comrades as a loner, often flying singly, and on the ground he built himself his own hut away from the others on one aerodrome, so that he could be nearer to his machine. His off-duty time was spent tending a small garden and practising the violin. Although not anti-social *per se*, he was none the less extremely shy and sensitive. One of Nottingham's most revered sons, Ball was a wily tactician. By spring 1917, however, he was reaching the nadir of his career on the Western Front. With forty-four confirmed victories, a DSO with two bars, a MC and finally a VC (posthumously) and all before he reached the age of 21, Ball inspired numbers of other young men to join the RFC. In action, he attacked with seemingly reckless ferocity, diving straight into groups of enemy fighters. His religious conviction gave him a sense of calm in battle, believing that if God wished him to survive then he would do so. In an interview he stated,

> One has to be patient and practically live in the air if one wants to account for a lot of German airmen. Several times I have gone up after them in such a hurry that

> I haven't had time to put my clothes on – being clad only in my pyjamas. It was jolly cold, I can tell you. The German airmen know my favourite dodge pretty well I think, but somehow they have not yet stopped me from making it effective. The dodge is a simple one. When I get to close quarters I generally pretend that I am going to attack from above. The Hun gets ready to fly up at me, and then I dive under his machine and empty a drum into his petrol tank and down he goes.[3]

Ball met his fate on 7 May 1917, but not before he had inspired another of Britain's greatest airmen, who around the same time was just beginning his flying career. Major Mick Mannock would go on to become one of the highest scoring aces on the Western Front. Later in 1917, Sergeant Rigger Edward Davis of Gillingham was responsible for looking after Mannock's aircraft in No. 74 Squadron. Previously Mannock had borrowed a cigarette, and now before heading into action, he threw Davis his own full cigarette case. Such was the affection and admiration that Mannock inspired among his ground crew that it was still one of the ex-rigger's proudest possessions forty years later.

There are many accounts of the awe in which the pilots of the RFC were also held by the troops on the ground. In one instance in April 1917 an Australian infantry officer, Captain Harry Lambert Wheeler, having witnessed a dogfight above the lines, was instructed to write to Major W.H.C. Mansfield, who led No. 20 Squadron, regarding the incident:

> Dear Sir,
>
> the Commanding Officer has asked me to express a deep sense of admiration which was inspired by the gallant flying of an airman, apparently belonging to a squadron under your command. About 6 pm on the evening of the 7th instant two of our planes were engaged with nine of the enemy's. One plane was damaged and the other, although retreat looked possible, turned and fought. Several of the enemy's planes scattered, but unfortunately our plane was hit and immediately burst into flames. The scene was witnessed by the men of this battalion from the trenches, and the conspicuous bravery was much spoken of by them. The gallantry is sure to foster a spirit of emulation for our men to strive hard, on their part, to act in the same heroic and self- sacrificing manner as this gallant airman. The true bravery of your fine Corps was thus strikingly brought home to our men.[4]

The officer in question was Captain Mahony-Jones who, with his observer Lieutenant William B. Moyes, returned to assist Lieutenant Lawson whose F.E.2 had been hit and was in trouble. Through their sacrifice, Lawson was able to return safely to the British lines.

By spring 1917, however, the increasing losses being sustained by the RFC as it continued to keep the pressure on the Germans (particularly in support of the new offensive on the ground at Arras) were impossible to ignore. In what was to be called 'Bloody April' the situation had reached its nadir. The statistics certainly make for sobering reading with something like 316 pilots and observers killed or missing in April alone, and 224 RFC machines destroyed in the same period. The superiority of recently introduced German fighters, principally the Albatros DIII, contributed greatly to this situation, which was compounded by the 'vicious circle' effect, that as more pilots were lost, replacements were rushed out to France with perhaps inadequate training and therefore more likely to become casualties themselves. Second Lieutenant Harold Balfour was flying a Sopwith 1½ Strutter with No. 43 Squadron and remembered,

> Most of our casualties were with fairly new pilots. They couldn't keep formation. We used to say that if your engine was not giving full power, if for some reason you couldn't keep up, put the nose down and get below us and you'll be comparatively safe because, what we did when the German circus dived on us was, we just went round in a circle. We were two-seater fighters and all the observer's guns in the circle were concentrated on the diving Germans. We gradually edged the circle (each chasing each other's tail) towards our lines and with any luck we'd get over. Sometimes with casualties, sometimes without. They were very trying, very hard times. Trenchard came round the squadron and we thought he was going to tell us how sorry he was for our casualties and what fine chaps we were. Not a bit of it. He said, 'You never finished your job, get on and do more than you are doing' and very nearly told us all off.[5]

Paradoxically, Balfour recalled that this did more for morale than if Trenchard had made a maudlin and sentimental speech about casualties. There was no doubt, however, that COs felt the pressure. On 29 April 1917, Lieutenant William Norman Hamilton of No. 19 Squadron, RFC was flying a Spad on an offensive patrol between Douai and Cambrai. He reported later that,

> Major Harvey-Kelly leading sighted and attacked Richthofen's (?) circus 14 strong over Epinoy. Lieut Applin (the third pilot) was shot down at once and killed. Circus split up, half on the Major and half on me. My gun gave repeated No. 4's and eventually a No. 2 not before I had shot down one Hun. My gun jammed hopelessly over Douai so I made for the line having lost the Major (who was shot down & died three days after in a German hospital). Both my tanks were holed and I had to land.[6]

As a squadron commander, Harvey-Kelly should by rights have not been in the air; his duty was to remain on the ground overseeing the operations of his pilots, but on that day he had heard that von Richthofen was in the area and decided to join the patrol.

With death so apparently arbitrary – and so commonplace – it is little surprise that talismans and charms came to be imbued with great superstitious power.

> 'It's becoming positively childish', said the Major, as a small aviator passed the window with a large silver mascot

dangling from his identity bracelet, and turning with a frown to an orderly told him that he wanted to see Mr. McGuy, then he sat down at his table and prepared for an offensive. Ten minutes later McGuy came out of the office looking worried, and the bracelet on his wrist was conspicuous by the absence of ornament. McGuy looked unhappy for the greater part of the evening, and before going to bed unburdened his sorrowful soul to Jimmy. 'It's too childish for words', he said, unconsciously reiterating the Major's words. 'She only sent it to me two days ago – anyway, I'm going to carry it with me to-morrow [*sic*].' Words failed him, and Jimmy looked appropriately sympathetic. McGuy, with an angry glance at the sky, retired to his hut to brood in solitude over the foibles of superior officers.

Before getting into bed he placed with tender care two small objects on the table by his bed. One was a silver bulldog with enormous bulging eyes and a large smile; the other was a locket. Before turning out the light he opened the latter and looked for a few moments at the photograph within, and turning over on his side nestled his head in the pillow and was soon asleep. McGuy was just eighteen and very young for his age – or was he old? One never quite knew.[7]

In the flat plains of Flanders, RFC observation balloons took the place of hilltops as a means for observation over enemy lines. Originally observation balloons were of the spherical design but these had a tendency to twist around on the mooring rope, and it was essential that the observer be able to maintain continuous observation on a fixed point. For this reason, the kite balloon came into being. The shape of these offered resistance to the wind and they remained more or less stable. Nicknamed 'Ruperts' they were raised and lowered on a cable wound in by a motor winch tender. The balloon held between 30,000 and 50,00cu ft of hydrogen, enough to lift the car holding the two observers with all their maps and equipment, plus parachutes. Balloon observers were the only RFC crew routinely provided with these, and they were expected to jump if the balloon came under serious attack by enemy aircraft. This was by no means a guarantee of survival, however, as the blazing balloon might come down on top of them.

The riggers or ground crew were responsible for the daily inspection of ropes and replacement of frayed ones. The riggers also supervised any topping up with gas, which might be required and carried out checks on the valve. If a large amount of topping up was required, the 'nurse' balloon was used. Small amounts only were taken from gas cylinders. Because of their highly explosive nature, the cylinder dump was usually located some distance away, and lugging the heavy cylinders around was an unpleasant task. Because they were so closely attached to the artillery, the balloons were often sited on ground that had previously been churned up by horses and limbers, further adding to the misery of their crews. Because balloons were frequently attacked by enemy aircraft, the ground crews were provided with two Lewis guns and a Vickers machine gun. The ground crew were as much at risk as the observer if enemy aircraft attacked, because they were expected to stay at their posts both to winch the balloon down, and to provide defensive fire from the machine guns. The risk of the burning balloon coming down on them was also a distinct possibility.

A remarkable and unique set of double gallantry medals was awarded to a balloon observer, Flight Sergeant George G.L. Blake. Firstly the DCM was awarded in June 1917, this citation reading,

> For conspicuous courage and determination while observing from a balloon, which was brought down by hostile aircraft. Though injured, he immediately ascended again, and was once more shot down. This N.C.O. has rendered valuable services at all times.[8]

Blake was subsequently commissioned, and received the Distinguished Flying Cross (DFC), this citation reading,

> Throughout the recent operations this officer has rendered most valuable service in face of heavy hostile fire and attacks by enemy aeroplanes, compelling him on three occasions to parachute. He has completed 470 hours in the air, displaying gallantry and initiative of a high order.[9]

William Robinson Clarke, the first Black pilot in British service, started his career in France as a driver with an observation balloon company. With the outbreak of war,

Clarke, one of the first men to learn to drive in Jamaica, paid his own passage to Britain and joined the RFC in 1915. Clarke wanted to fly, however, and in December 1916 he was accepted for pilot training in England. On 29 May 1917, Clarke, now a sergeant, joined No. 4 Squadron RFC at Abeele in Belgium and began flying R.E.8 machines over enemy lines. While on a reconnaissance mission on the morning of 28 July 1917, he and his observer, Second Lieutenant F.P. Blencowe, were attacked by enemy fighters. He described the action in a letter to his mother:

> I was doing some photographs a few miles the other side when about five Hun scouts came down upon me, and before I could get away, I got a bullet through the spine. I managed to pilot the machine nearly back to the aerodrome, but had to put her down as I was too weak to fly any more ... My observer escaped without any injury.[10]

Despite the shortage of aircrew at this point in the war, there was a reluctance on the part of the authorities to accept non-white recruits from the British Empire. An exception to this rule was made for Hardit Singh Malik, a Sikh who had studied at public school in Britain before progressing to Balliol College, Oxford. When, like his contemporaries, he had tried to enlist in the British armed forces upon the outbreak of war, he was at first denied a commission. Only the intervention of one of his Oxford tutors secured Malik a cadetship in the RFC. By summer 1917, he was a qualified pilot and would go on to claim two kills before he himself was shot down. His Sopwith Camel was found to be riddled with over 400 bullet holes but he survived and would go on to become Indian High Commissioner to Canada, and Indian Ambassador to France.

In July 1917, Air Mechanic Alfred W. Gray, an engineer from Coventry in civil life, was posted to No. 43 Squadron, who were in the processing of exchanging Sopwith 1½ Strutters for Sopwith Camels. It was his first overseas posting, and it was a tedious journey to reach them via the No. 2 Aircraft Depot at Candas. This involved a long, slow ride on the French railway system. The train was filthy, with no internal doors, the seat upholstery ripped and the floor thick with the remains of army biscuits, bully beef and even carelessly lost rifle ammunition. When he eventually reached the squadron however, he discovered that the sprit and camaraderie was good from the start. He was slightly apprehensive when he entered the canteen for the first time but was met by a large banner hung across one end, exhorting all in foot-high capitals to 'SMILE DAMN YOU, SMILE.'

His first week was spent in the workshops of HQ Flight, getting to know the innermost details of the Clerget engine, which powered the Camel, and understanding what adjustments needed to be regularly made to it. Then he was paired with a rigger, Davis and the two were detailed to an aircraft of their own. Between them they kept it in good order, helping each other where necessary. The fuel capacity of the Camel enabled it to stay airborne for about three hours and if it had not returned in this time an aircraft was assumed either to have been shot down or landed elsewhere. Two patrols a day of one and a half to two hours were usually flown by each aircraft, unless a major offensive was underway. One flight would get airborne just as another was about to return, in order to provide continuous cover on the squadron's sector. After an aircraft returned the pilot was asked about its performance. If the engine was running well and the rigging good, any minor battle damage was quickly repaired, and the aircraft refuelled to go out again. More serious damage meant that the aeroplane was taken to a hangar, for the workshop tradesmen to assess if it could be repaired on site.

Gray remembered that the interrupter gear was a constant source of trouble on the Camel. As the machinery suffered from wear this could create a time lag, also differing qualities of cordite in the .303 ammunition used could affect the velocity of the bullet, so it was not uncommon for a stray round to hit the propeller. Gray actually changed one propeller that had been hit by seven bullets in one blade and four in another. Captain John Trollope MC served with this squadron, and later in the war Gray and some other mechanics were sent to guard his aeroplane when it force-landed in fog. A local farmer gave them shelter and provided hot coffee.

An example of the ingenuity required of RFC ground crew comes from Air Mechanic R. Davidson, of No. 18 Squadron. Around this time, one of the squadron's F.E.2b machines was shot up and crashed near Peronne, some 60 miles from the squadron's base. Davidson flew out to inspect it with the squadron's new CO, Major (later air vice marshal) Ranald Reid. The damage consisted of both main spars of the top centre section, engine cylinders and oil tank shot through, but it was thought possible to bring the machine back to airworthy condition. A new wing section, engine and oil tank were drawn from squadron stores, and transported to the crash site. The ground crew had earlier established a procedure for replacing the 12ft-long top centre section, without dismantling the mainplanes. Davidson takes up the story,

> This involved supporting the aeroplane with trestles under the front and rear of the nacelle, one under the tail and one under each wing tip. As the upper tail booms were fastened to each end of the rear spar of the top centre section, you will realise that when this wing section was removed the balance of the plane was very precarious until the new section was in position. Fitting the new engine was straightforward, except that, being short of manpower I had to borrow four German prisoners-of-war and, as a result of the language difficulties I thought (at one time) the engine was going to topple over, so we manhandled it into position. We finished the repairs in about 2 ½ days and the plane flew back to the squadron.[11]

By this stage in the war, coordination between ground and air forces had reached a high degree of sophistication within the BEF. Aircraft located hostile artillery, and directed British guns on to them, in order to suppress them during an infantry attack. One pilot, Captain Sylvester Quine, serving with No. 21 Army Cooperation Squadron, RFC earned a MC this way, the citation describing how he went out in rough and stormy weather during an attack, and flying low over the enemy batteries reported and located those that were in action. In a letter of 17 October 1917, he describes this mission:

> I was up on another 'nasty job' today but it turned out quite well as it happened. I had another 'bus' from our flight escorting me and he stuck on splendidly. Old 'archie' [anti-aircraft fire] got very excited and fair hurled hate up at us but didn't do any damage. Then three Huns dropped down out of space and came for us. I saw them a good way off so opened up with my front gun and made some decent shooting. Then I let the observer get a shot in but his gun jammed. The Huns however didn't feel like a fight after that …[12]

His letter goes on to describe a rowdy concert in the squadron officers' mess that same evening, perhaps a way of unwinding after the tension and drama earlier in the day. By 1917 the war in the air was becoming a struggle that tested men and machines to their very limits. In the case of air crew, the effects were both physical and psychological, though the latter was poorly understood at the time. As a result, there was a growing body of evidence of combat stress among air crew, but little official consistency about what to do about it. One only needs to consider contemporary attitudes to shell shock among the infantry to realise that medical knowledge of mental health, and of what today is termed post-traumatic stress disorder (PTSD), was extremely limited. Most of the contemporary medical literature is concerned solely with what made for the characteristics of a good pilot, rather than any wider analysis. One medical treatise at the time came up with the blindingly obvious assertion that marriage was unlikely to contribute to making a good combat pilot, because of the added sense of responsibility that it would bring. Another reflected the general attitude towards 'loss of nerve' among pilots:

> It is certain that an aviator's disinclination to fly must have its basis upon some temporary defect of mind, and, without being unduly sensitive or timid, he should realise this and overcome the cause rather than tempt Providence by running the danger of over taxing his power.[13]

Combat stress, the loss of comrades, limited opportunity for relaxation and long hours in an open, noisy, unheated cockpit all took their toll. The authorities were certainly aware of the impact of continuous combat operations on individuals and their effectiveness, and consciously chose to limit the length of observers' tours of duty. For them, the maximum was six months at the front. Indeed, it has been suggested that as many as 50 per cent of pilots suffered from serious neuroses during operational tours. Even so, the medical establishment remained uncertain as to what to call the condition. Various terms were used, such as 'fatigue', 'flying stress' or 'Flying Sickness D', which applied to aircrew neurosis involving anxiety, hysteria or depression.[14]

There can be no doubt that for numbers of observers in particular, the repeated exposure to danger had a corrosive effect on morale. One former pilot, E.L. Williams wrote,

> I had several air fights, mostly unsatisfactory. Once I was attacked by two enemy scouts and my observer cried like a child and refused to fire, though they fired about 200 rounds at us. Foolishly I did not report this as I rather pitied his terror, which was akin to my own but more wantonly and stupidly expressed.[15]

Perhaps the most severe case of combat stress was that of Second Lieutenant Robert Cameron, an observer with No. 9 Squadron flying in R.E.8s over the Ypres Salient. The unit was on army cooperation duties and provided support to infantry attacks, photographic reconnaissance, as well as artillery registration and counter-battery work. Cameron was posted to the squadron on 10 September 1917, at the height of the Third Battle of Ypres. The fighting was so intense that more than one of the squadron's aircraft was actually struck by a British artillery shell while in flight. The squadron record book shows that Cameron was involved in four crashes in this period (two in September and two in October 1917) all of which wrote off the aircraft involved. Not all of these incidents were necessarily due to enemy action, as the squadron's base at Proven had a notoriously difficult approach, but between October and November 1917 his machine was attacked three times by enemy aircraft, which he fought off with his Lewis gun.

On 7 January 1918, Cameron was on patrol over the Ypres Salient when he took his own life by spontaneously jumping from the aircraft at 1,000ft. Whilst we cannot say for certain that his suicide was caused by combat stress, the circumstantial evidence makes it seem likely. A Court of Enquiry was convened a few days later to look into the circumstances of his death, which reached no firm conclusions, except for the fact that the pilot was not at fault. However, various witnesses testified to the fact that Cameron's effectiveness had deteriorated as the months had passed; he had been drinking heavily, and he had not gone to bed sober the night before the incident. On the morning that it happened, he was pale and confused. Perhaps to spare his family further pain, his CO recorded his death as killed in action.

Front line squadrons had no full-time medical officer; these were only to be found at wing level, the squadrons only possessed an enlisted medical orderly, who could provide first aid but was not even allowed to administer morphia. Serious casualties were evacuated by stretcher. In this situation the first person to spot weakening morale was usually the flight or squadron commander, the latter of whom could return an officer to home duties if he felt that he was becoming a liability. At least some however had a 'robust' attitude to mental health problems among their aircrew, and the 'stiff upper lip' outlook was prevalent. One officer, Squadron Leader Glenny, wrote after the war,

> Nowadays, a crash creates a great deal of stir and alarm, the pilot and observer have to go to a medical inquisition and as often as not are recommended to a short rest if they are not seriously hurt. During the war a different spirit prevailed and I recollect that the principal was to step out of the remains of one aeroplane into a whole

> and flyable new one. To my mind the war idea is much sounder and I often think that many cases of 'nerves' one meets nowadays among beginners may be down to the present system.[16]

The effects of long-term exposure to danger and fear were not solely confined to the British side of the lines. It has been suggested that Manfred von Richthofen was suffering from PTSD at the time he was shot down, and the memoirs of Ernst Udet, who took over von Richthofen's mantle as Germany's top scoring ace after his death, wrote candidly about his psychological battles in his memoir *Ace of the Black Cross*:

> Very soon he was so close that I could see the observer's head. With his rectangular goggles, he resembled some great, ferocious insect bent upon my destruction. The moment had now come for me to shoot in earnest, but I was quite unable to do so! It was as though horror had turned my blood to ice, taken the strength from my arms, and numbed my brain. I sat passively in the cockpit, flying straight ahead, and staring idiotically at the Caudron as we passed each other. 'You miserable coward!' the engine seemed to say. I had failed miserably at the crucial moment. I had thought of myself, and had trembled for my own safety. There and then, I vowed to rid myself of the stain that now lay upon my honour.
>
> The moment had come. My heart beat furiously, and the hand which held the joy-stick was damp. My Fokker flew above the enemy squadron like a hawk singling out

> its victim but did not pounce. But even as I hesitated, I realised that if I failed to open the battle immediately, I should never have the courage to do so afterwards. In that case I would land, go to my room, and then, in the morning, Pfalzer would have the task of writing my father that there had been a fatal accident while I was cleaning my revolver.[17]

Udet, like many pilots, fought against feelings of sympathy for and anxiety about his victims. After one aerial victory he wrote,

> I flew back to the aerodrome, my skin soaked in perspiration, and my nerves in a desperately excited state. I had made it a rule never to let myself worry about the men I shot down. He who fights should not look at the wounds he inflicts. But I felt an insatiable desire to know who my opponent had been. I made my way to the scene of the crash. My opponent had been shot through the head. The doctor handed me his wallet: Lieutenant C.R. Massdorp, Ontario, RFC 47. Also in the wallet were a picture of an elderly woman and a letter. It said: 'Don't be too reckless. Think of father and me.' Somehow one had to try to get rid of the thought that a mother wept for every man one shot down.[18]

In the early part of 1918, observer Walter Noble was flying with No. 20 Squadron operating Bristol Fighters. He concluded that the stresses endured by air crew were many times greater than those suffered by their comrades in the infantry:

> Nerves are sooner or later developed by all who fly. But not for some time after they have made themselves felt on *terra firma* do they appear in actual flying. It is the anticipation of unpleasant incidents that generates fear. In contact with them all is forgotten in the struggle for self-preservation ... later, when, metaphorically speaking, the nerve germs have bred sufficient white corpuscles to overcome the healthy red ones, fear begins to assert its sway when up aloft. The victim is now in a state of perpetual intense excitement, masked by an outward semblance of calm; and the wise and observant Squadron Commander decides that it is time another of his officers went to Home Establishment for a rest.
>
> I am sure that men undergoing equal strain and suspense on the ground would not last so long. The Infantry will probably not agree; but I, too, have been in the trenches, and have come to the conclusion that the actual nerve strain endured by them bears no comparison to that to which airmen are subjected. Remember in Fighting Squadrons (and it is to them that I refer) one goes over the top as it were once or twice on all except very 'dud' days and sometimes three, four or more times. Always there is the certainty of a vociferous welcome from Archie, and in most cases there is a scrap.[19]

By New Year, the weather over the Salient had turned particularly cold. It was so bitter in fact that it began to hinder aerial operations. Observer Lieutenant George Fuller wrote of a sortie on 3 January 1918,

> I never suffered so badly from the cold; one of my cheeks was frozen by the time we landed. I certainly had taken all the measures that I could to combat the weather; heavy woollen underwear, silk socks underneath wool socks, slippers (I think these were of the ladies' bedroom variety) with leather soles lined with felt and woollen uppers, overshoes, silk gloves under combination leather gloves with adjustable fur lined mitt to cover fingers, Sidcot suit, woollen balaclava helmet under my fur-lined helmet, and face mask and goggles, both lined with fur.[20]

In these conditions engine radiators froze, some even on the approach when the engine was throttled back, but most commonly after a night out in the open. As a precaution against this, radiators were usually drained at the end of flying. Coppersmiths came into their own, repairing burst radiators and blanking off the most vulnerable parts. Pilots were instructed to keep revs up as high as possible on landing, but the problem was not solved until manually controllable radiator shutters were fitted.

Robert Mckinley Jamison was a veteran of the 36th Ulster Division, who had already seen a good deal of combat on the ground. With the casualties that the infantry had suffered in the previous year, it became necessary to amalgamate his battalion. As a result of this blow to his sense of unit identity and *esprit de corps*, he felt compelled to answer a call for volunteers for the RFC, and in February 1918 was accepted for training as an observer. He was posted firstly to a school for infantry and artillery cooperation, where the curriculum included Morse code and machine gun training, plus seven hours flying experience, then on to a school of aerial gunnery where he accrued a further five hours flying, thus with only twelve hours of experience he was posted to an operational squadron. There was little glamour attached to the vital but dangerous reconnaissance work that he was about to undertake, which often involved flying straight and level while photographing enemy positions. On arrival at the squadron he reported to the flight commander, Captain Norman Goudie, a no nonsense Canadian who took him up for his first mission. As soon as they crossed the enemy lines the firing started from below. Jamison returned fire on the enemy trenches with his machine gun, to little effect. Shortly afterwards the true nature of their sortie became apparent. He wrote,

> [Goudie] started sending Morse. I noted that he used his fist on the sending key. He called up a siege battery to begin a pre-arranged shoot on a German battery, and for the next three hours he conducted this operation. We were in the air from 11am to 2.10pm … later in the day we were again in the air at 4pm on another pre-arranged destructive shoot, returning at 7.10pm. Thus ended my fist day in No 5 Squadron, in the commanding presence of a backwoodsman from Kamloops.[21]

The aerodrome that the squadron used in 1918 was at Acq, near Vimy Ridge. Here they operated R.E.8s. Built in Britain by the Royal Aircraft Factory, the R.E.8 (Reconnaissance

Experimental 8) was a two-seater multi-purpose biplane with forward and rear-firing machine guns. It was first introduced into RFC service during late 1916 and used in artillery observation and night bombing roles. The aircraft was nicknamed the 'Harry Tate'. More than 4,000 R.E.8s were built during the course of the war. Although it was claimed to have a synchronised forward-firing .303-in Lewis gun and one or two Lewis guns on a Scarff ring in the observer's cockpit, there were variations in the R.E.8. For example, in some cases a Vickers .303 would be fitted. Also, many incidents occurred where ammunition being fired ahead would damage propellor blades. The Scarff ring in the observer's position was supposed to make handling the guns easier and give support. To a certain extent this was true, but the R.E.8 was not a highly manoeuvrable aircraft, and when trying to follow the track of an enemy aircraft, it was quite a heavy cumbersome task swinging Lewis guns from one side of the cockpit to the other to get a sighting on target, even if mounted on a Scarff ring. The Scarff gun mount was supposed to be a mechanically operated interrupter gear, which prevented the gunner firing at the propeller. In practice, in the field the locking nuts would loosen and the ball joints would wear, causing miss-timing of the gear and consequent damage to the propeller. Air mechanics were responsible for the maintenance of the gear, and if propeller damage could be traced to bad workmanship on their part, a court martial could result.

The early aircraft were prone to spinning, resulting in a number of accidents and the R.E.8 was grounded while a larger tailfin was designed. The maximum speed of the aeroplane was 102mph, and service ceiling was at 13,500ft. Rolls-Royce suffered a production shortage of their 'Eagle' aero engine, which resulted in most R.E.8s being powered by the 150-hp Royal Aircraft Factory 4a air-cooled twelve-cylinder in-line motor, though some received the 200hp RAF 4d engine, and others had a Hispano-Suiza power unit. It was a great relief to the crew, that the engine's exhaust outlet extended over the upper wing, so that the crew members were not exposed to exhaust fumes. Bomb load on the R.E.8 extended to 224lb. Although the R.E.8 eventually shared, and accepted, the role of bomber, like other early aircraft its initial value was seen as simply an extension of the army. Not surprising, as it had emerged from Royal Engineer roots, and was expected to immerse itself in range-finding for Allied guns and evaluating enemy troop movements; all these duties placed a heavy responsibility on the observer.

No. 5 Squadron were the sole occupants at Acq and could conduct artillery spotting within sight of 'home'. If damaged or wounded in action but still airworthy, crews could get quickly to base and receive attention. It had, however, an uneven surface, disliked by the pilots and by the R.E.8 aircraft. If an R.E.8 encountered a bump on the ground on touching down, she invariably bounced like a startled hen. On the next, or subsequent bounce the tail would come up and she would bury her nose, after which she either stood on her head or carried on with the revolution, right over onto her back. As the observer could not be strapped in due to the nature of his trade, all he could do was tuck himself in, and wait for the appropriate moment to crawl out and release the pilot who hung upside down on his safety belt. He invariably fell headfirst onto the grass.

As the squadron patrolled its 'beat' daily between Lens and the Scarpe river, they were fair game for the von Richthofen *Jagdtstaffel*, whose lair was a few miles on the other side beyond Douai. Many of its aeroplanes were shot down by this hunting pack. This was accepted as part of the job, but after some nights of intermittent shelling and consequent loss of sleep and some casualties and damage, the squadron pulled out and was installed in a new, already overcrowded station at Izel-le-Hameau, now out of shelling range. Jamison remembered,

> Scarcely had we settled in when we were discovered and a visitation in the shape of a night bombing attack was made upon us. The four squadrons sharing the aerodrome with us were ignored. We got the lot. I was sitting in my collapsible rubber bath in three inches of water, well soap lathered, when one of the 'visiting cards' dropped at the door of my hut. The door and windows blew in. The candle blew out, my 'do-it-yourself' ceiling of soot laden boards tumbled down. I emerged from the collapsed bath covered in soot and soap suds. After a dry shampoo I put on my pyjamas, donned flying coat and boots and soot streaked as any commando, headed for the nearest hangar. It was burning furiously and flames from it were licking our hut. Petrol tanks exploding and ammunition going off all round, there was little we could do here. Unfortunately one bomb dropped on the sleeping quarters of the ground staff, killing 13 and wounding many more. The other

> squadrons soon arrived and gave great help in attending to the trapped, wounded and dead.
>
> Our flight commander, the redoubtable Capt. Goudie, was mad with rage. As dawn broke he was all set, and off we went with myself in the observer's cockpit. I was still in pyjamas and still streaky. We headed for the aerodrome at Douai and we caught them unawares. They were wheeling out the aircraft from the hangars in preparation for the day's flying. We straffed them at ground level, dropping 20 lb bombs and machine-gunned them all and sundry till our ammunition gave out. And so home. Leaving a trail of dead and wounded and two aeroplanes burning. Thereafter we were left in peace, although trenches were dug around the huts. These were never used and the only minor 'casualty' resulting was when 'Red' Webber, a Canadian, returned from leave in a state of elated inebriation, fell into a trench outside his quarters and spent the night there sleeping peacefully.[22]

Jamison's flying logbook recorded 160 patrols in which he took part. Many of these were the 'daily round and common task type.' They consisted of counter battery patrols, reporting enemy movements, directing artillery fire on active German batteries, counter battery area photos (a 'dicey' job), destructive shoots on pre-selected targets and gun positions, night reconnaissance, contact patrols during attacks by British troops and counterattack patrols when he could call enormous artillery fire on the attackers' infantry and artillery. During all this the observer could never allow himself to forget for a moment that 'the price of liberty is eternal vigilance' for the temperamental old R.E.8 was not designed or equipped to either fight or run away. When forced to fight, he recalled that they took their toll of enemy single seaters. As for running away: well on the pilot's dash board was a small printed notice – 'Do not drive over 110mph.' If he did so, his wings were likely to fold up. There was good humour among the men of the reconnaissance squadrons, but for all that they took their job seriously. There was pride and a determination in the RFC, qualities that saw them through to the war's end.

Another young observer freshly arrived in France was Second Lieutenant Roy Shillinglaw. He had been a pupil at a minor public school and had been inspired by the sight of a French pilot landing his aircraft on the playing fields before the war. It was no surprise that when in 1917 a recruiter from the RFC visited the school, he enthusiastically volunteered. Two days later his papers came through, and he was ordered to report to Farnborough for training. One month after his nineteenth birthday, in spring 1918 he was posted to France. His first operational unit was a bombing squadron based near Nancy in Lorraine. He takes up the story,

> This was 104 Squadron and I was surprised to be there because I had been trained for night bombing. I found the machines were DH9a's which had American Liberty engines (reputed to be unreliable) and single flying wires on the wings which meant that if one was hit, the wing fell off! Furthermore, the petrol gauge was on the left, level with the pilot's head. This was a glass tube and

> directly above the exhaust. If this was hit, down went the machine in flames. However I was a fair shot with rifles and machine guns and felt this was just my cup of tea and what I wanted and would make the best of it. In the mess that evening after dinner I found I knew many of the pilots and observers for we had trained together. They started playing 'Slippery Sam'. I saw cheques for £50, £100 and even £250 flying around, so I said to a friend, 'What's the idea?' for £250 was equivalent to a year's pay. He replied, 'What does it matter for we shall all be dead in a week as we are being shot down like flies.' I thought what a real hot shop this is, but 'in for a penny, in for a pound', this is what I have come out for, to hit the Hun.

The following morning, twelve machines from the squadron set off to bomb the railway station at Karlsruhe. Shillinglaw went to the aerodrome to watch them return, but saw only four machines land:

> They lifted a dead observer out of each plane and started swilling out the cockpits with buckets of water. That squadron was 18 machines strong and was wiped out three times.[23]

That same day the adjutant informed him that he should be with No. 100 Squadron, so he was transferred by car to Ochey near Nancy, where he arrived about 4.00 pm. This place was where, on 4 March 1918 the unit had been posted, to form the nucleus of the Independent Force under Major General Hugh

Trenchard. He was given a map of the area and by 9.00 pm that evening he was airborne, and on his way to drop two 40lb phosphorous bombs on a target at Boulay. Most of the time he flew in F.E.2bs and was assigned to the machine flown by E.C. Middleton. Shillinglaw regarded him as an excellent pilot, who was not afraid to go into a target, and who would perform all sorts of evasive manoeuvres if caught in the cone of a searchlight. He continues:

> I was not strapped in and my cockpit was roomy, for the observer on an FE2b had to move about using the Lewis Gun, and bombsight and release bombs and three minute flares in a slot in the floor of the cockpit. When the machine was upside down, I used to sit on the floor with both legs from the knees downwards outside the cockpit, and grip the edge with the back of my knees and at the same time grip the gun post with both hands and hold on. Middy never seemed to think I might fall out![24]

Despite the open cockpit and intense cold, Shillinglaw recalled that they were often bathed in perspiration after combat, or after getting clear of a target:

> It certainly wasn't fear but apparently a cold sweat resulting from intense concentration. One rarely felt fear – we were too young to do so! – though I think everyone without exception had a tummy ache an hour or so before take off; no doubt due to anticipation of

> what was to come. How fortunate we were in comparison to the poor devils in the trenches who were in constant mud and under shellfire. We at least had a tablecloth and a bed and dry conditions.[25]

There were difficult moments, undoubtedly. One came when he went up on a raid with a new and inexperienced pilot; some 40 or 50 miles over enemy territory they met a German fighter, which the gung-ho youngster was keen to engage:

> I had to explain to him we were heavy with bombs and our job was to deliver them, which we did. I then shone a flashlight on the bomb racks, checking that all the bombs had gone. I carried a long cane, clipped to the side of the plane to knock off any odd bomb which may have failed to release. In doing so I noticed that one landing wheel had been shot off. I suggested to the pilot he bring the machine in at 45mph air speed which was just in stalling speed. Instead of which he brought it in at 60mph, ran across the drome on one wheel until we went over and spun on our nose. I was thrown about 20 yards landing on my hands and knees unhurt.[26]

By this stage in the war an RFC squadron in the field had a bewildering array of trades among the air mechanics, all necessary to keep the unit functioning efficiently. Attached to every flight there was not surprisingly a fitter and a rigger for each of the aircraft, but also armourers, a blacksmith, a sailmaker for the repair of aeroplane fabric, a coppersmith for work on fuel pipes and small metal fittings, a storeman, a welder, a compass swinger and an electrician. There were also officers' batmen, motor cycle dispatch riders, men to drive and maintain the squadron's Leyland lorries and Crossley tenders, as well as a driver for the CO's Crossley touring car. In the Headquarters Flight would be found cooks, clerks and a telephonist. A two-seater squadron would of course require more cooks and officer's batmen and might also include a wireless or photographic section, which would require manning.

For a rigger, wings, struts controls and wires were his responsibility. Bad weather, which reduced flying time, gave crews a welcome respite from the hard monotonous work of re-rigging and adjusting the many wires and struts of an aeroplane, which was required after each flight. Other men might have to patch bullet holes in the wings with Irish linen fabric stuck on with dope, the distinctive smell of which was not easily forgotten. Some engines were known to liberally spray castor oil behind them and this would cover the lower wings, resulting in drag. This oil would have to be laboriously cleaned off after every flight. An Air Mechanic 2nd Class earned 2 shillings a day, and an Air Mechanic 1st Class earned 4 shillings per day, which was still less than the wages earned by the squadron lorry drivers (being able to drive at this time was still quite an uncommon skill).

Engine maintenance required other specialists, and the facilities for working on them depended on the circumstances in which the squadron found itself. Each Flight carried two spare engines, making six in total for a squadron. At any time four had to be serviceable so that only two were in the workshop at any one time. A logbook was kept for each engine, and after a set number of flying hours for each type, it would be removed from the airframe by the Flight fitters. This could be an awkward procedure depending upon what lifting tackle was available at the airfield. The same team would then fit the replacement engine but other, workshop, personnel would undertake the overhaul of the removed item. If the work required on the engine was beyond what could be achieved at the squadron, the task had to be carried out at the RFC's Engine Repair Shop (ERS) located at Pont de l'Arche on the Seine. Henry Albert Marsh was a fitter at No. 1 Aircraft Depot at Marquise. He remembered,

> The engines were made at ERS … that's where they stripped the engines that had done their time, and they used to repair them, then box them up, then send them to us. We had the frames, and we put the engines into the frames, and they were taken out and tested on the aerodrome, and then sent out to the squadrons. Working conditions were not bad, we were in Bessonneau hangars, whacking great hangars, terrific size, probably hold about twenty or thirty planes. We had all the tools, winches and heavy lifting gear to get the engines on to the frames, and then the riggers came and they worked on it and you got the finished article out. We were tired because we worked long hours, when the big [German] push was on [in spring 1918]. The Air Mechanic First Class was an ambitious young man, he wanted to be a corporal, and he pushed us.[27]

For most RFC ground crew, it was a relatively safe existence at airfields behind the lines, or perhaps aircraft parks even further back. For a few, however, it was a life almost as dangerous as that of their counterparts in the air. Any parts from a crashed aircraft that could be salvaged had value, particularly instruments, machine guns but especially the engine. A typical aero engine would have cost over £1,000 in 1918 prices, and teams might be sent considerable distances to try to recover one if it was known where a machine had crashed. Sergeant Horace Waters would be better known in later life by a stage name, as the actor Jack Warner, of 'Dixon of Dock Green' fame. Now however he was a No. 12 Squadron motor driver on the Western Front. He recalled,

> … as a driver [I] had to ferry wireless operators to and from the lines. I think I can claim to be the only driver who got his Crossley tender balanced upon the edge of one of the second line trenches, at a place called Monchy-le-Preux, which many old soldiers will remember. I ended up like that on a night of heavy shelling when I lost my way, and I didn't realise what a highly precarious position I had reached until the whole area was illuminated by flares. At the time I was a flight-sergeant and engaged on a special mission which entailed going up to the front line at all hours to salvage engines from aeroplanes which had been shot down. We were always on call and one night I had just got my head down when with two or three other chaps I was summoned to the C.O. for a special briefing. We were

> shown a map and ordered to the front line just beyond Arras to drag one of our aero-engines back to the lines. It was a hazardous operation in thick fog and, ironically, it was only German flares which actually enabled us to reach the engine we wanted. It was no picnic and we were very relieved when our mission was accomplished.[28]

For these operations, Waters was to be awarded the Meritorious Service Medal. It was during the war however that he also had a taste of showbusiness, when with a group of other air mechanics he formed a concert troupe called 'The Aerolites'. He wrote a lot of the material for the performance, including some of the jokes. Such concert parties were a major source of entertainment for the troops in France and had a significant effect upon morale. Waters remembered,

> I discovered that some of my humour seemed to be acceptable to the lads, who wandered into our shows utterly exhausted and with their nerves in shreds after too many weeks in the lines.[29]

On 1 April 1918, the RNAS merged once more with the RFC to form the RAF. At the end of December 1917, just before the Air Ministry took it over the RNAS comprised 2,741 aircraft and 6,920 engines with personnel of 87,815 officers and other ranks, operating from 45 aerodromes, seaplane stations and shore establishments. The success of the RNAS contributed to its own undoing. In competition with the RFC, it scooped the cream of the output from the aircraft factories. To ensure more equitable distribution the Air Board came into being, and from that sprang the RAF. Frank Courtney remembered,

> If the birth of the Royal Air Force produced a vast commotion in political and administrative circles, it passed almost unnoticed among the flying men, whether on the field of battle or at home. The war still raged, and the change didn't make it look any different. We had heard a lot about what our new sky-blue uniform was going to look like and, faithful to tradition, we found nothing about it to praise. We ridiculed the bananas on the cap badge, we sneered at the brass buttons that would liken us to doorkeepers, and we would miss our Sam Browne belts, that unmistakable trademark of the officer. But most of all we shuddered to think that the proud letters 'RFC' on our wings would now be replaced with 'RAF', which hitherto had been the label for the dismal planes and engines of the Royal Aircraft Factory. The Factory would slide out from under that unloved designation by changing its name to Royal Aircraft Establishment.
>
> The official uniform of the RFC had been the double-breasted, high collared 'maternity jacket', infinitely smart and dashing but really quite uncomfortable, and too warm in hot weather or indoors; mostly we wore the usual infantry jacket. Now we discovered a belated affection for our old, distinctive garment. Outside of staff offices, few bothered to hurry into the new uniform, perhaps it seemed to proclaim too loudly the end of the RFC.

> It was at the naval air stations that the shock of the change was more immediately felt. The new Royal Air Force adopted army titles of rank; the present distinctive titles would not be invented for some time yet. Navy traditions being what they have always been, it was a dreadful thing for a Navy Captain to have to call himself a Colonel, or for a Lieutenant Commander to become a Major. The nautical lingo of a naval air station had to be revised to conform with landlubber vocabularies, and the distressing effect on old time Navy men was enough to bring tears of compassion to a visitor's eyes.[30]

In fact, the new RAF chose not just to follow army nomenclature but specifically to follow cavalry traditions (for example with trumpeters, rather than buglers) and totally eschewed any vestige of its naval heritage. The creation of the RAF from the merger of the RNAS and RFC might have passed off with little comment in the squadrons on active service but it threw into focus a conundrum that had been in question for some time, specifically the relative positions of pilot and observer in the operational hierarchy. In the RFC, the unwritten rule was that the pilot was always the more senior member of the crew. This prejudice was reflected in the significantly greater number of gallantry awards made to pilots, and it obviously still rankled with some former observers many years later. George Fuller, for example, who flew with No. 9 Squadron, remembered,

> On every flight the reports of duties carried out ... were written by the pilot and handed in to the Squadron

> Office ... some of them certainly needed no press agents ... If the observers had been given the same opportunity they might have picked up a few more mentions [in Despatches] or perhaps the odd decoration for their part in a joint effort.[31]

This was not an isolated opinion, for James Stedman in recalling his time with No. 100 Squadron in 1918 wrote,

> .... my pilot was awarded an MC for his work and the CO told me he was recommending me for one, but I was not to be too hopeful because the theory was that observers did not need to be brave: they just went where their pilots took them. So I did not get it.[32]

The Admiralty, in considering the role of its observers had accepted that these people might be eligible to hold executive rank and had set the ceiling as high as captain in the RN. The RFC had never set a policy on this matter, but clearly it was necessary to bring these mismatched approaches into line in the new service. It was, therefore, decided by the Air Council that, in order not to damage the promotion prospects of anyone who had come from a RN background, to round up, rather than down. At a meeting on 1 May 1918 it was decided that, subject to having to undertake a brief flying course, all RAF observers were eligible to reach the ranks of flight, squadron or wing commanders. The response from senior officers in France, however, was one of dismay. Both Trenchard and Salmond protested that any such appointments would seriously damage the efficiency and morale of the RAF in the field. Never the less, the Air Council upheld its earlier decision, and by the end of the war there were signs that deep rooted attitudes were beginning to change. In part at least this developed in the Independent Force, whose long-range missions required the presence of a competent navigator. Had the war continued, the heavy bombers in development might well have been captained by such a navigator.

Corporal A. William 'Bill' Sainsbury was actually still a member of the Wiltshire Regiment, when he had been seconded to the RAF as a probationary aerial gunner with No. 48 Squadron. On the morning of 3 May 1918, he and his pilot Captain Alexander Claud Garden Brown boarded Bristol Fighter C814 (which was normally the mount of squadron commander Major Keith Park, who would go on to Battle of Britain fame.) Some 60 miles to the north-east, at an airfield just outside Lomme, near the Franco-Belgian border, Paul Aue, an offizierstelvertreter (warrant officer) in the Imperial German Air Force, was also similarly preparing for take-off. His single-seat Pfalz D.IIIa was armed and fuelled, and with two wing wardens, one on either side, giving him a running start to get the plane airborne. Aue had been being seriously injured in a dogfight above Roulers, Belgium, the previous September, and had been grounded for eight months. This was his first mission since returning to combat duty.

Aue was already an ace. Before his injury, he had scored five combat victories, including a British SPAD S.VII brought down over Belgium in June 1917. He belonged to Jasta 10 – an elite German air squadron whose thirteen aces were feared for their skill and accuracy in battle. That day he was accompanied by five other planes, maintaining a loose formation as they headed south-west toward the front. Cruising in the vanguard, Aue probably tested his LMG 08/15 machine gun by firing a few rounds.

At just gone noon Brown and Sainsbury were circling in their F.2B above the French village of Proyart. Sainsbury was on the lookout for movement on the ground, but it was from the air that danger came when, on the horizon, six dots approached from the north-east. The British pair must have known that the odds were not in their favour. Minutes later, Aue shot down Brown and Sainsbury over German-occupied territory. The 'Bristfit' had been in the air for ninety-five minutes, before the machine came down in a controlled crash landing. Both airmen were listed as missing, and Brown was to die of his injuries three days later. Inside the twelfth century St Peter and St Paul's Church in the small village of Mottistone on the Isle of Wight, a memorial on the wall is dedicated to Brown who 'died of wounds received in aerial combat' in Herleville, France, on 6 May 1918. It states: 'Though mortally wounded himself, he effected a landing, thereby saving the life of his observer.' He was 27 years old.

Sainsbury, wounded and presumably pulled from the plane by German soldiers, was subsequently taken as a PoW. He was initially transferred 3 miles south-east to Herleville and then to a PoW camp in Guben, Germany, now on the border with Poland. He did not find out that Brown had died until several weeks later. In Guben, he saw out the final six months of the war working in the parcel office in a camp populated mostly by Russian prisoners. A local newspaper announced his return to England in February 1919, three months after the war ended. Family testimonies state that he came home a changed person and depict him in later life as a detached and introverted man who worked as a postmaster in a small corner shop and rarely left his home town. The image contrasts greatly with that of the young man in airman's uniform. His physical injuries must have lasted as long as any mental anguish that he suffered, for at the time of his death in 1966, he was still drawing a military disability pension.

In August 1918, No. 100 squadron had converted to Handley Page 0/400 heavy bombers and, therefore, longer-range sorties over industrial sites in Germany became possible. The squadron conducted these raids throughout the rest of the war; an aircraft from the unit was the last in wartime to return to base (on the night before the Armistice) from a raid. Shillinglaw remembered,

> I didn't enjoy flying very much in the Handley Page. Walking across from our hut to the machines we looked almost like Father Christmas in a Sidcot flying suit, flashlight with battery in a box slung around one's neck and a pile of maps under one's arm. I always took with me a small Gladstone leather bag containing a gross box of Nestle's chocolate (in case one was down on the other side and needed food on the run), half a dozen bars of soap, spare socks and shoes and a razor.

> With this bag the chaps gave me the nickname of 'maternity doctor' but I didn't mind their chaff. At the end of the war I had been on about 40 raids with 100 Squadron but they are not all recorded in the 'annals'. For instance, I think I was in the last machine to land at 2am on the morning of November 11 (war ended at 11am). We had been to the Mannheim area and on landing found all the squadron celebrating and 'pickled' and the orderly room was closed, so there was no record.[33]

Lieutenant Robert H. Reece also flew with No. 100 Squadron on night bombing missions and left a highly detailed description of the airmen and their aerodrome, in particular the map-room next to the squadron office. If a squadron on active service could be compared to the human body, the map-room was the brain of the squadron. Here was kept all the information essential to the aviators. On one wall was a huge map of the war zone from the coast to the Swiss border. On this the front-line trenches were accurately marked, with changes updated daily. On the wall next to this map, was a large-scale plan of the entire region over which the squadron operated. On this map were numerous markings, with no meaning to the casual observer:

> In maps of the enemy territory are hundreds of red drawing-pins. These mark the positions of enemy anti-aircraft batteries. As soon as information is received of

the movement of one of these batteries, the pin which represents that particular battery is moved to the new position. Small yellow squares or oblongs with minute black marks represent the enemy aerodromes and hangars. These conventional signs correspond accurately to the aerial photographs of these aerodromes.

Small blue crosses represent the position of enemy balloon barrages and their height. The position of these barrages must be known accurately, for to run into them is fatal and at night they are very apt to trap the unwary. Roughly, they are a series of balloons supporting a huge wire net or cable streamers. The balloons, anchored to the ground and carrying the nets with them, are sent up to a considerable altitude about large cities and important industrial centres. They are to the night aviators what the spider's web is to the fly.

Another conventional sign of this map which is always puzzling to the uninitiated is a series of small pins with streamers attached. These streamers are marked with green dots. One streamer will have one green dot, another two green dots, another three, etc., while others will have different spaces between the dots. These pins mark the position of what is called the 'Hun green-ball batteries', and these green balls, fired up to a height of about six thousand feet, direct the Hun aviators to their respective aerodromes when returning from a night raid.

A better system than this for directing aviators at night has never been devised, for low clouds or mist cannot obliterate the signal and they are visible to the aviator for

> over fifty miles. In fact, this type of signal was so very excellent that our knowledge of the exact positions of the various batteries was of great assistance to us in our raids over Germany.[34]

Another squadron that operated the giant machines was No. 97, based at Xaffer-Villiers, which became operational on 19 August 1918. Among the observers here was Second Lieutenant Albert Griffiths, one of the few who had first volunteered as an air mechanic, and had then subsequently received a commission, despite his lowly upbringing. He remembered that the airfield was a grassy field surrounded by trees, lit by acetylene lamps at night. He recalled some frightening take offs as pilots struggled to clear the trees while laden with bombs: 'They were so slow those planes. With the wind behind us the fastest speed we ever recorded was 145 mph.'

Part of the observer's job was to plot the course for the night, usually a mission to a railway yard or factory in the Mannheim area. After that, he manned a machine gun in case of enemy attack. Once over the target he lined the aircraft up for bombing, crawling through a trapdoor into the nosecone of the aeroplane, directing the pilot onto the target with hand signals, then pulling the bomb release cord. One night after releasing the 250lb device he found that the trapdoor was stuck. He started to climb out over the nose to get back to the cockpit:

> The pilot saw what I was doing and deliberately banked the plane, throwing me back into the fuselage. He saved

> my life. I would have been whipped away in another few seconds.

On the return journey he would usually release smaller bombs from the side of the fuselage onto the enemy trenches below:

> We came in fairly low and we could often see the German soldiers shaking their fists at us. The lads would also be waving as we crossed our own trenches. Looking back, it all seems so primitive now. We always liked to smoke a cigarette on the way home and I would literally take the wheel while the pilot lit up.

A few weeks before the Armistice came one of the most difficult missions. Returning from another night raid over Germany, the plane had an engine smashed by ground fire. With no parachutes, the crew faced a harrowing journey back to base that night:

> We had a few close shaves and that was certainly one of the closest. My log book afterwards simply recorded three terse words: 'port engine conked'.[35]

In September 1918, Second Lieutenant Ralph Silk, formerly an infantry officer, joined No. 6 Squadron as an observer. He was to take part in more than fifty operations, not all of them recorded in his logbook. As he acknowledged later in life, he started off recording each operation, but eventually there just was not time; between 14 October and 23 October 1918, he was averaging two or three sorties per day. Shortage of aircrew was an acute problem, but his spiritual beliefs helped to sustain him:

> I'm very religious. I used to say my prayers every night before I went up. It certainly helped. We'd already lost a lot of pilots and observers in the squadron. On this particular day I'd already been up twice, and I was absolutely exhausted. Then our squadron leader said I'd have to go back up again, there was no one else. I suddenly thought: I'm not coming back this time.

Silk and his pilot, Lieutenant Ralph Cresswell, set off again but were soon set upon by a squadron of German aircraft.

> We hadn't a chance. They came at us over the sun, and the next thing I knew, the machine lurched and the pilot was lying dead on the controls. Of course, we went into a spin. I don't remember much about the fall.[36]

The aeroplane's descent was broken by a group of trees into which it came down. Unconscious, Silk was disentangled from the wreckage by German soldiers who took him to a church. He came round several hours later, the sun shining through the partially broken windows cast the shadow of a cross on the wall. It seemed to be an omen and affirmed that it was his religious faith that had saved him. After treatment in hospital, he was taken to a PoW camp in Germany. Meanwhile, Major G.C. Pine, CO of No. 6 Squadron, had written to his mother:

> As yet, I am sorry I have no information about your son. He was out on photography and was brought down by EA … my observers think there is every chance that your son would be alright. We are now getting near the ground over which the flight took place. I hope I may have better news soon. I do hope he may be alright, as he was a very good observer, and is a great loss to the squadron.[37]

Air Mechanic P.S. Swain had been a garage mechanic in civilian life and had hoped to be employed in the same role in the RFC. Instead in its wisdom the corps employed him as a motor lorry driver, and he spent the first period of his service collecting the remains of crashed aircraft. Later he achieved his ambition by transferring to a flight engine mechanic but his only training course was in the United Kingdom on the Sunbeam Arab engine. Mechanics were expected to pick up knowledge on other types whilst on service. When No. 22 Squadron converted to Bristol Fighters, there were a number of teething troubles that mechanics had to overcome. Engine maintenance consisted largely of cleaning points and plugs, and fixing oil leaks. The fitters also found that trueing up was more critical on these high-performance aircraft. Late in 1918, Swain was posted to No. 16 Squadron, an artillery spotting unit flying R.E.8s and based at St Eloi. The Germans were now retreating and the squadron, moving up behind the advancing Allied front, took over a former enemy aerodrome at Auchel. They housed their aircraft in the wooden German sheds, but these had been extensively bombed, and the aerodrome huts and hangars leaked through innumerable small shrapnel holes.

The wings of the R.E.8s became waterlogged, and after heavy rain the underwing fabric of the affected aircraft had to be opened up to let the water out and was then repatched.

By now, the Germans were in obvious disarray and the end of hostilities appeared imminent. RAF units were some of the first to learn the news of the impending Armistice through their access to radio equipment. Air Mechanic 2nd Class Thomas Aldridge remembered,

> I was a Wireless Operator stationed near Lens at the time [of the Armistice.] I had arranged some home-made coils to my then crystal set, to increase its range so that I could get the 'news broadcasts' from Poldu in Cornwall (in morse code only then.) It enabled me to obtain early information that an armistice was being negotiated. It was about midnight, and I rushed into the billets to spread the good news to our chaps, only to be sworn at for waking them up. What gratitude![38]

At all levels there was an awareness of what had been achieved by the air arm in four years of conflict, but for many there would now be uncertainty about what the future held. For the hostilities only men, the question was how quickly they might be demobilised. For those for whom the armed forces had been their career before war began, what prospects might there be for them in a RAF, which was certain to undergo a reduction in strength from wartime to peacetime footing. For some, there would doubtless be opportunities in the burgeoning world of civil aviation.

Chapter Five

Mediterranean, Aegean and the Persian Gulf

Almost from the outbreak of war, RNAS and RFC units had provided air support to military operations in theatres away from the main European battlegrounds. In time these would come to be known as 'the sideshows' – campaigns whose outcome could do little to influence the main decision being fought out on the Western Front. Never the less, each brought with them their own unique challenges for pilots and ground crew attempting to operate flying machines, and to take the war to the enemy.

Air Mechanic 1st Class Leonard Callow of the RNAS, from Tunbridge Wells, had been engaged since March 1915 in balloon observation work at Gallipoli. He and his comrades rendered the fleet and army invaluable service in discovering Turkish positions and giving the range. In this direction they materially aided the landings of the Australian troops, and they had on several occasions forced the *Goeben* to hide herself behind land (for fear of being destroyed by British battleships), and thus prevented the German warship from firing on Allied troops or transport. The dreadnought HMS *Queen Elizabeth* was able to destroy several Turkish batteries after being given the range by the officers and men of the RNAS, and they were cooperating with HMS *Triumph* at the time that vessel was torpedoed. The Balloon Air Service also assisted materially in connection with the landing at Suvla Bay. Callow and his comrades' most exciting experience was perhaps when an enemy Aviatik appeared and rained bombs around them, without, however doing any serious damage.

The balloon was moored from HMS *Manica*, a former manure-carrying vessel from the Manchester ship canal. There was only one trained observer in the kite balloon section, Squadron Commander J.D. Mackworth, but as kite balloons could stay up all day, and the observer was in constant telephone communication, thus a target could be continually observed. From the point of view of naval gunnery this offered advantages over aeroplane observation, though of course a balloon could not reach the same height as an aeroplane, could not operate on windy days, and as well as the risk of interference from the air as described above, there was also the danger of submarine attack. HMS *Manica* was particularly vulnerable, as she carried the flammable gas for the balloons in her hold. Once the potential for explosion was realised, this gas was transferred to a tender, the tug *Rescue*.

HMS *Ark Royal* had been active in support of the Gallipoli operations since the last days of February 1915. Operating initially from Tenedos, the senior flying officer of the ship was Captain Cecil Francis Kilner who was present at the bombardment of the Dardanelles Forts from 17 February 1915 to 12 March 1915, the attempt to force the Narrows on 18 March 1915, the air raid on Smyrna, and the landings at Anzac and Suvla in April and July 1915. Another of her seaplanes was piloted by Flight Lieutenant Geoffrey Bromet. In his diary for 17 February 1915, he writes of a wireless trial at a maximum height of 4,500ft:

> Before returning to base we dropped two bombs – one at Kum Kalessi which found its mark and one at Seddel Bahr which fell short. The enemy opened fire on us with field guns, rifles and machine-guns, but only managed to hit us seven times ... the flight lasted for 1 hour and 15 minutes.[1]

Great care had to be taken with the machines, as new aircraft and even spare parts would take six weeks to arrive from Britain. Bromet was very conscious of his dependence on the efforts of his mechanics, writing,

> CPO Finbow worked solidly on a difficult and annoying job for sixteen hours and I cannot praise him or Air Mechanic Somner too highly for their painstaking and successful work and for their cheery optimism throughout.[2]

In April 1915, HMS *Ark Royal* was reinforced by the arrival of No. 3 Squadron RNAS under Commander Charles Rumney Samson, who had established an aerodrome on the island of Tenedos. This had been built using Greek labour, rent being paid for the ground and compensation for the vines that had to be dug up. The large Farman biplanes were landed in packing cases, and in a laborious operation these were hauled on rollers by labourers and sailors up the slope from the shore to the new aerodrome. While the officers lived in a small house or tents, the empty packing cases provided accommodation for the other ranks. Other airfields were constructed at Imbros, Mitylene and Rabbit Island. More aircraft would arrive later (including Nieuports) but the Maurice-Farman pusher type biplane, powered by a Renault engine, provided the backbone of land-based aviation in the Dardanelles.

Samson was the outstanding personality in the field of aviation in this theatre. Short, stocky and irascible, his fury and intemperate language were quickly roused, and he suffered no fools under his command. Pilots were always to be armed with a pistol, observers with a rifle and both were to familiarise themselves with the profiles of Turkish men-of-war in *Jane's Fighting Ships*, a copy of which was kept in the squadron office. Short but accurate reports he considered to be more important than verbose ones. His confidence in himself comes across clearly in his private writings. On 19 April 1915, after hitting a howitzer with a bomb, he wrote, 'I was very pleased with myself, especially the first gun, as it was the result of a careful sighting shot.' He flew over the Gallipoli landing beaches on 25 April and recorded,

> Wonderful sight and I will never forget it … corpses on the beaches and the blood in the water were sights that made you feel rather rotten sitting up there aloft with nothing to do except spotting the ship's fire … The water was simply whipped into foam by the shells and bullets … the Q.E. [HMS *Queen Elizabeth*] was putting salvo after salvo into the town … you could, from the air, trace the tracks of the shells passing through the houses before they burst.[3]

In the early summer, Turkish positions and troop movements were regularly harassed by the dropping of bombs and also bundles of flechettes, small metal darts, to which the Turks objected even though the German Taube aircraft that were supporting them also made use of these items. Ships and submarines were also bombed, and torpedo attacks were launched from the newly arrived seaplane carrier HMS *Ben-my-Chree*.

HMS *Ben-my-Chree* was chartered by the government on 1 January 1915. She was one the fastest vessels in the British coastal services, and it was perhaps for this reason that she was converted to be a seaplane carrier. This was done by Cammell Laird at Birkenhead, and considerable changes were made to her superstructure, with a large hanger for the housing of seaplanes being added to her after deck along with cranes for lifting seaplanes on and off the vessel. In May 1915, HMS *Ben-my-Chree* was despatched to the Dardanelles, in order to participate in the Gallipoli campaign. Her aircraft were engaged in spotting targets for the guns of the big battleships, which formed the Eastern Mediterranean fleet. She saw considerable action during this period of her service; she was more than once the subject of a torpedo attack, but being of shallow draught, the torpedoes passed underneath her. The Official History of the campaign considered HMS *Ben-my-Chree* particularly valuable as a mobile self-contained air unit, and on 12 August 1915 she became part of aviation history, when she was the platform for the first ship-launched airborne torpedo attack on an enemy vessel. One of her aircraft sank a Turkish transport vessel in the Sea of Marmara, after it had flown right over the Gallipoli Peninsula in order to reach it. The pilot, Flight Commander C.H.K. Edmonds, reported that, as he looked backwards,

> I observed the track of the torpedo, which struck the ship abreast the mainmast, the starboard side. The explosion sent a column of water and large fragments of the ship almost as high as the masthead ... she appeared to have settled down a little by the stern when I ceased watching her.[4]

However, there was no real air-to-air combat over the Gallipoli Peninsula. Although the presence of German aircraft is frequently mentioned in contemporary diaries, they were too few in number, and individually too ineffective, to cause much inconvenience to the Allied troops below. The German bombs were only of 20lb weight, many were duds, and none caused serious damage. Flying conditions in this theatre were almost perfect. Until late autumn it was possible to fly at any time of day, and every day. Although visibility was good, pilots and observers were hampered by the fact that on the Gallipoli Peninsula there were few easily distinguishable geographical or man-made features, and maps were insufficiently detailed or accurate. The thick scrub afforded easy concealment to troops on the ground, and the terrain was as confusing from the air as it was at eye level. The improvised Turkish anti-aircraft fire became more effective as the campaign went on, resulting in the loss of several Allied machines. There were further problems in that observers were untrained, wireless telegraphy gear was often inadequate, most aircraft were not fitted for carrying wireless equipment and the majority of fittings had to be made locally. Only the seaplanes of HMS *Ark Royal* had wireless telegraphy sets at the outset, and though equipment was later installed in land-based planes it was often unreliable.

An aerodrome was established at Cape Helles as early as 30 April 1915, and aircraft were based there in pairs for daylight operations. However, as it was always under Turkish observation, they did not as a rule remain there overnight but flew back to Tenedos. From 30 June 1915, Turkish fire became so heavy and destructive that even this limited use was abandoned and the Helles landing strip was thenceforth only used in emergency. One of the men who manned the aerodrome, Leading Air Mechanic Beeton, of No. 3 Aeroplane Squadron RNAS, felt compelled to write to the secretary at his former boys' club:

> … to tell you candidly I have no particular desire to die just yet. Some people think that the flying service is a safe number, but I can tell you otherwise. Yesterday for instance, I was helping to dismantle a machine under shell-fire on the Gallipoli Peninsula.[5]

A dummy aircraft placed here in October attracted some 650 enemy shells. Sub-Lieutenant Bell Davies described the yellow fog through which occasional landings at Cape Helles had to be made, when the prevailing north-east winds blew the dust off the sun-scorched and dried Gallipoli Peninsula:

> At the landing ground one had to turn without being blown over and taxi hastily downwind to the spot behind the mound before the Turkish shells arrived.[6]

On 19 August 1915, an aeroplane, piloted by (now promoted) Captain C.H. Collet DSO, RMA was ascending from Imbros aerodrome, and had reached a height of 150ft when the engine stopped. The machine was upset by the powerful air currents from the cliffs, and fell vertically to the ground, while the petrol carried burst into flames, which immediately enveloped the aeroplane and pilot. Collet was a remarkable man. He was known as the Marine with the photographic memory, so accurate that he could play chess blindfolded. This incident deeply affected Samson, who wrote,

> [Collet] was burned to death. His loss was a terrible loss to the squadron, and I lost a great friend, he was absolutely irreplaceable. Chief Petty Officer Keogh, Jones and Robins displayed remarkable bravery in attempting to save him.[7]

In fact, Keogh was to be awarded the Albert Medal for this incident (later exchanged for the George Cross), the citation reading,

> Chief Petty Officer Keogh, upon arriving at the scene of the accident, at once made an attempt to save Captain Collet by dashing into the midst of the wreckage, which was a mass of flames. He had succeeded in dragging the fatally injured officer nearly clear of the flames when he was himself overcome by the burns which he had received from the blazing petrol.[8]

Flight Lieutenant Bromet left the Aegean in September 1915, but before he did so he revealed in his diary some of the tensions that existed between the seaplane pilots and their shore-based counterparts:

> People laugh at sea planes and ask what use are they. Why? Because they have only experienced and been able to compare the work done by *Ark Royal* (whose hard work had to be carried out with seven seaplanes of an inferior quality and with no spares) and Cmdr Samson's squadron (whose aerodrome we built and had ready when he arrived) of ten or more land machines supplemented by new ones when necessary. I allow that as things have worked out aeroplanes can do the [Gallipoli] Peninsula work better than we can, but one must not forget that the naval front extends from Enos right down to Smyrna and that had the campaign gone as it was expected to go aeroplanes would have been of little use owing to the necessarily rapid changes of aerodrome.[9]

In November 1915, Bell Davies and another officer named Smylie set off on a mission to destroy the railway supply route from Bulgaria at Ferijik Junction. In the action, Smylie's aircraft was damaged and he was forced to land in Bulgarian territory. He destroyed his aircraft by means of the bomb that it was still carrying, and as enemy soldiers were approaching, Bell Davies landed beside the burning wreck to rescue his comrade. The aircraft was only fitted with one seat and Smylie had to squeeze under the engine between the rudder bar and the engine bearers, with his head periodically bumping the oil tank. So tightly wedged was he that when the plane finally reached the safety of Imbros, it took the air mechanics two hours to disassemble the machine sufficiently for him to be extricated. Bell Davies was awarded the VC for this action. In his memoirs, he left a detailed description of the living conditions at Imbros, created from an aircraft packing case divided into three rooms:

> The two end rooms we fitted with bunks and used as sleeping cabins; doors connected with the middle room which we used as a sitting room. Wash basins were made out of petrol cans fitted on hinged brackets which shot the dirty water outside. Windows were made from the glass of old photographic plates. We improved the oil drum stove by building a proper fireplace in our sitting room with fire blocks and fire clay looted or rather salved from the old colliers which had been sunk to form a breakwater for the small-craft anchorage in Kephalo Bay. For fire bars we used tappet rods from wrecked gnome engines. In fact we were as well housed as possible to face a Gallipoli winter.[10]

Flight Sub-Lieutenant F.D.H. Bremner of No. 2 Wing RNAS was one of the last to use the Helles airfield in January 1916 and recorded in a letter that although his engine was misfiring, he flew towards something noticed by the observer to the north of Krithia. On returning, their plane was,

> Attacked by a Hun who came up unobserved behind and slightly above me. Did not know he was there till

> he started firing and even then did not realise at once what it was. As soon as I did realise I attempted to turn left to bring my Lewis Gun to bear on him and just caught a glimpse of him over my left shoulder. He then disappeared behind me and again fired a few rounds, and apparently made a big right-handed sweep and made off in the direction of Chanak. He was too fast and nippy for me to bring my gun to bear on him, and the whole thing only lasted about thirty seconds![11]

Bremner attempted to follow but finding that his engine revs had dropped realised that he must have been hit and would not be able to reach Imbros. Instead, he made for the Helles airfield. He cannot have been a welcome guest, because by then the evacuation of the Gallipoli Peninsula was in its final stages. With the aid of some mechanics he and the observer tried to push the plane into a dugout, but it would not fit and had begun attracting Turkish fire. Eventually it was decided to smash it up with picks and a sledge hammer. Bremner and his observer left the Gallipoli Peninsula with the troops being evacuated and were soon back on Imbros taking part in a RNAS hockey match. Young officers like these received much encouragement from Wing Commander E.L. Gerrard, who was now commanding the unit, and he was shortly to be awarded the DSO for his personal example and leadership.

In late 1915, a new seaplane base had been constructed by the RNAS at Kalafrana on Malta, using material originally intended for the construction of huts at the Dardanelles. A slipway and seaplane hangar were built, and the base operated

Felixtowe F3 flying boats, mainly on anti-submarine patrols in the Mediterranean. Although most of the 100 or so Felixtowes that were constructed during the First World War were built in Britain, about eighteen were assembled locally in Malta. Local craftsmen built the hulls, and Maltese women sewed the fabric. These aircraft were supported by a number of DH.9 bombers that operated from the Royal Malta Golf Club. With the formation of the RAF, a group of independent flights on Malta were brought together to form No. 267 Squadron. Among the seaplane carriers that operated in Maltese waters was HMS *Manxman*. She had been built for the Midland Railway, and in peacetime operated their route between Heysham and Douglas. After requisition by the Royal Navy, she was converted by addition of an aft hangar. Like other similar coastal steamers, she was fast and ideally suited for launching seaplanes.

HMS *Ben-my-Chree*, whom we met last in the Eastern Mediterranean, was to meet her fate in early spring 1917. She was the last warship to withdraw from the Dardanelles, when the Gallipoli adventure was finally abandoned in January 1916, and had spent the time since providing mobile air support to Allied operations in the Middle East. Life for those on board was not entirely unpleasant during the two years she was on war service. She had a piano, and an orchestra, which gave concerts for the crew and also for visitors when in port. The hangar, when the seaplanes were removed, made for a fine concert hall, capable of accommodating about 400 people. The crew also had their own football, hockey and cricket teams and often played against local sides when in port. Captain William Wedgwood Benn joined the vessel in 1916 and remembered,

She was a new fast tripper recently built to do the journey from Liverpool to the Isle of Man. As that passage was a short one, the bunker accommodation in the ship was of a scanty kind by no means fitting her to cruise about for days, especially as her consumption of coal was commensurate with her fine turn of speed. To adapt her to her new work, a certain number of the cabins had been converted into coal bunkers, and in addition when long trips were made, as, for example, down the Red Sea, the decks as well had to be piled with fuel. Add to this the fact that the forced draught blew the dust through the lids of the coal holes in the deck and it will be seen that except in port, when she was a shining model of beautiful cleanliness, our ship was apt to be somewhat grimy. Aft of the funnels there had been a large deck or hall, once used, I believe, as a tea pavilion, and it was this which was converted into the hangar in which five or six machines – folded, of course, and in case of the single seaters, with the tails taken off – could be stored. We carried Shorts (two-seaters) and Sopwiths. Aft of the hangar was the launching deck with bollards, derricks, and steam winch.

The ship's company was split up between the airmen and the seamen. It is surprising, although we were a naval unit, how distinct, even divisive, was the class-consciousness of these two groups; though nothing in the least disturbed the magnificent *esprit de corps* which made the old *Ben-my-Chree* an imperishable memory for those who ever had the privilege of sailing in her.[12]

Her skipper at this time was now Charles Rumney Samson. Having returned to the Mediterranean, HMS *Ben-my-Chree* was lost in February 1917, while on patrol off the coast of Asia Minor, searching for Turkish gun batteries. She was in harbour at Castellorizo, an Island held by the French at the time, when a salvo was fired from a Turkish battery on the enemy-held mainland. The *Ben* was hit immediately, the explosions puncturing her petrol supplies. Burning petrol ran down on to her lower decks and she was quickly ablaze. Valiant efforts were made to extinguish the fire, but with her steering gear crippled as well, after half an hour the order was given to abandon ship. Wedgwood Benn remembered,

> I was resting in my cabin on the upper deck at half-past two when I heard a tremendous explosion and saw a column of water rise not fifteen yards from the ship. I was not surprised, for I imagined it was just the first of the usual two or three shots from an ordinary Taube [German aircraft], to which during the last few months we had been getting quite accustomed. The first explosion, however, was followed quickly by two real smashers, neither of which, so far as I remember, hit the ship. I went to find Samson; it was clear that something more than a mere aeroplane attack was in progress, and our minds turned to the battery, the presence of which the French had suspected some months before. I found the CO on the main deck quietly giving orders; he was in no doubt about the source of the attack. Just as I reached him, a shell, which must have been the third or fourth,

set fire to the hangar. Nothing now could prevent the ship from burning, and as further hits occurred, huge scarlet flames and masses of black smoke poured from the vessel. A few moments later the petrol store was hit and with it the fate of the ship was sealed. We were, of course, an actual 'sitter' for the Turks.

Direction and range offered no difficulty to their gunners; they could see us and our position relative to the town and could measure us off to a millimetre, and shoot simply from the map. Some minutes after the first attack a shot hit the whaler and swept it clean away; the bow was left dangling from one davit like a leg of mutton. In the meantime 'fire stations' had been sounded and the whole ship's company, except the crew of the twelve-pounder, was engaged in trying to quell the outbreak.

The gun was manned in the perfectly vain hope that it might make some reply to the 6-inch Howitzers, which had us in hand. The rest of us meanwhile were very busy dragging hoses into the hangar with the intention of putting out the fire; but flaming petrol is not extinguished with squirting water and it was soon clear that we were finished. We had steam, of course, and could have left the harbour, but what was the use of going to sea in a furnace with half a gale blowing, amid the certainty, at the best, of having to beach the ship on the Turkish coast and lose all the crew? Bitter as the decision was it was clearly the right one when the commanding officer ordered the quarter-master to pipe 'Abandon ship'.[13]

Fortunately, all 250 crew were able to escape safely and there was no loss of life. It was said that immediately after the war she might have been salvaged, but her former owners, the Isle of Man Steam Packet Company did not want her back – her fast speed meant that she was simply too hungry for coal, and so she was towed to Italy to be broken up.

The vulnerability of the Suez Canal – Britain's life line to India and the eastern half of its empire – was becoming increasingly apparent as the war progressed, and as Turkish forces massed in Palestine with a view to capturing it. Following the visit of Lord Kitchener to Egypt, when he famously observed that the canal was protecting the troops rather than the troops protecting the canal, action against Turkish forces on the eastern side was stepped up. Reinforcements were posted to Egypt, and RFC strength here was increased. In December 1916, Air Mechanic 1st Class John Henry Peat, a clerk who was serving at RFC 5th Wing Headquarters in Egypt, was in frequent contact with friends at home through letters published in his local newspaper. In one he wrote of the difficulties imposed by the desert climate:

> Summer has departed, and with it that accompaniment of intense discomfort, the 'khamseen'. Which I described in a former article. The flies, pestering legacy of heart-hardened pharaohs, are, like the poor, always with us, and we still hear in the watches of the night the song of the mosquito, while many a comrade's face bears with the dawn silent, but eloquent, testimony to their

> activities. The testimony may be silent in its eloquence, but that does not apply to the victim, whose vocabulary is extensive and powerful.[14]

A few weeks later Peat's regular letter to his local newspaper gave an illustration of the thriving *esprit de corps* in this unit, at a dinner to mark both the festive season then upon them, and the recent arrival of his unit in Egypt. The menu contained five courses and was embellished with pen and ink drawing of various RFC motifs:

> Don't imagine that we imported a chef for the occasion. The preparation of the meal devolved upon our camp cooks – men who are more accustomed to motors than menus, though the result was such as to make one wonder if they had not missed their vocation ... one of the busiest of the cooks' assistants was a lively young fellow rejoicing in the patronymic of Brookes, prefaced by Jack. He, in normal times is engaged at the Simplex Motor Works, Sheffield ... I am one of a number who have recently transferred to the Royal Flying Corps, and on this festive occasion the 'transfers' were the guests of the 'originals'. In this and other matters the 'originals' have been so decent to the 'transfers' that as the proceedings were drawing to a close one of the newcomers ... delivered himself of the following couplet:
>
> 'We haven't seen much of the Flying Corps,
>
> But from what we have seen, we would like to see more.'[15]

Conditions in Egypt, certainly in the early part of the campaign, were particularly hard on mechanical equipment. Among other things, engines were susceptible to damage from the effects of dust and fine sand, which blew about the aerodromes, until mechanics devised elementary air filters that were fitted to the machines.

The British campaign in Mesopotamia (modern day Iraq) had begun as an attempt to secure oil supplies from the region for the Royal Navy. However the war, run from New Delhi rather than London, was characterised by mismanagement and poor planning. An understrength force had initially faced little Turkish opposition, and the ambition had grown to seize the whole of the country as far as Baghdad. British overconfidence had resulted in the disastrous loss of the town of Kut, and now the woefully under-resourced army known as Indian Expeditionary Force 'D' was committed to fighting a German-supported Turkish army along the Tigris – a land of harsh climate, blighted by disease and in the company of a hostile native Arab population.

For several weeks an attempt was made to supply the beleaguered Kut garrison by air and some 19,000lbs of food was dropped into the town, along with medical supplies, wireless equipment and mail. With a disposable load of only 150 to 200lbs per aircraft, a number of trips had to be made. Harassment by enemy aircraft meant that some British machines had to be detailed as escorts, reducing the amount that could be carried. Ultimately the attempt ended in failure.

In June 1916, the strength of the RFC in Mesopotamia was one skeleton squadron at the front and one Aircraft Park at the Base in Basra. There was also a kite balloon section of the RNAS under Commander Wrottesley. Such was the lack of labour at Basra, that nine new aircraft had been waiting a month to be unloaded.

Major John Tennant commanded an RFC detachment sent to reinforce No. 30 Squadron, the only RFC unit then supporting the army on the Tigris, but the Western Front had first call on machines and replacement pilots, and this was the most neglected of the 'sideshows'. He found that the Aircraft Park, at Tanooma, on the side of Basra harbour, was a collection of palm-leaf huts with a few iron-roofed brick sheds, surrounded by desert. Here such arrears of work had accumulated that it was hard to know where to begin, and the men who were left had little life in them. It was only possible to work in the hours of dawn, for by 9.00 am the sun was getting up, and any remaining energy was necessary for bare existence. A large percentage of the staff were sick.

The enemy's aerodrome was at Shumran, a few miles above Kut, his flying unit being manned by Germans and equipped with Fokker and Albatros machines. Hitherto their sky had been clear; with only an occasional old B.E., Henry Farman or Voisin to hinder them, their morale was excellent. To quote Sir Percy Lake's despatch:

> As regards aviation, the superiority of certain of the enemy planes over any of our machines in the matter of speed, combined with a large reduction in the number of our pilots (due to sickness partly attributable

> to overwork), enabled the enemy in May and June to establish what was very nearly a mastery of the air.[16]

It was essential to destroy that morale, as in order to fulfil the role of close cooperation with cavalry, artillery, and infantry, and carry on the photography and mapping of any area in the hands of the enemy, any air service must be in moral supremacy. The personnel of the squadron were severely under strength and most of them sick men, unable to leave their tents many days of the week. More machines were, however, got into commission, and would go out in the early hours of the morning hunting for Germans. The effort was not in vain, and within a week Lieutenants Lander and Barr shot down a Fokker that had come up from the Shumran aerodrome, and been previously engaged by another B.E., in which action Lieutenant the Honourable J. Rodney was wounded. After this, aerial combats were intermittent, and the enemy seemed to lose appetite for close action. There was yet another way to shake his morale; and with bombing raids he was harried in his lair by day or night. Tennant described the first of these:

> … time was allowed for the Turk to have his supper and get to sleep; he had never been bombed by night before, and we hoped that the surprise of this little jaunt might further its effect. Just after eleven Captain de Havilland left the ground with a cheery wave and was gone in the darkness; a few minutes later came 'Contact, sir!' from my mechanic, and I was away. Our course took us over

> the desert west of the river, which shone like quicksilver in the moonlight far to starboard. A strong head-wind made progress slow, but it was pleasant to be up in the cool vastness of the night above that strange country. It seemed ever so long ago that I had left England. A series of flashes in the distance ahead dispelled reverie; D. H. was attacking. Gliding slowly with engine off, I arrived short of the aerodrome at a height of 400 feet, when suddenly there burst a storm of heavy and concentrated rifle fire from what must have been at least a thousand rifles under well-directed control. It had been my lot during the war to come under fusillades of varying intensity, but this reception was perhaps the warmest up to date: the sound was like the tearing of a piece of calico. After dropping the bombs on the hangars my speed down wind gave the Turks small chance. Captain Herring, who had followed me, came in for a similar reception, but D. H. had surprised them as had been expected.[17]

The attackers returned home for a cheery 2.00 am supper by the Tigris, consisting of sardines and coffee, with the air mechanics who could not sleep for sand flies.

Many of the Arab tribes in the desert were hostile to the British, but one man's name carried great weight with them. Colonel Leachman was a political agent who lived among the Arabs, eating their food and dressing as they did, in effect a second T.E. Lawrence though lesser known. British flying officers were given his name printed in Arabic in large letters on a card, lest they be forced down in hostile territory. The army had both land and water transport at this stage of the campaign. On the river there were 100ft barges divided into the workshops, dark-rooms, stores, etc., essential to a flying unit. These barges remained or moved with their flights, for this was a river war, and the Tigris being the only artery of supply and communication the force could not move far from it. For land transport they possessed three light lorries, a Hupmobile car, and fifty-six Australian mules to haul six specially constructed waggons. This mule transport was the great pride of the RFC.

Wireless gear was fitted in all machines, and artillery cooperation practised and developed. By the end of August 1916, the work of registration of the enemy positions was in full swing. Great difficulties had been experienced by the force due to the complete lack of reliable maps. The only method of mapping a hostile country is by photography, and an extensive programme in this respect was carried out each morning, commencing with an area of 40 square miles round Kut.

Flying in the hot weather was a great strain, and, after service in France, it was odd to see a pilot going off for a long flight dressed only in shorts, stockings, and shirt, with a helmet bound down on to his head, for at 5,000ft the sun's rays are as fierce as on the ground. Throughout September, reconnaissance, photography, and artillery cooperation kept all available machines busy each day. A web of intelligence was being woven and added to that gathered by other means at Tigris Corps HQ. In a desert country with efficient aerial observation, it is impossible for an enemy to alter his dispositions without discovery; the movement of a few tents or shelters can be spotted at once, and there are no woods or buildings in which to hide his men.

The moral effect of the British aeroplanes was gradually growing; it must have been with eyes searching the horizon that any Turk or Arab column moved out into the desert. On 25 October 1916, a machine on reconnaissance observed a column of horsemen and mule carts moving south along the Hai tributary. The pilot came down low and dispersed the convoy in all directions. An agent later reported that nine were killed, several wounded, and that the carts, which were loaded with ammunition for Arab levies on the Hai, turned back to Kut after the attack.

Enemy aircraft were fairly active and commenced a half-hearted campaign against the British aerodrome at Arab Village; they dropped their bombs from a great height, and their shooting was inferior. Sometimes one dropping into the river would provide fish for the camp. The old B.E.s gave chase, but there was small chance of bringing them to action before they got down to their aerodrome at Shumran. Any raid was answered within a few hours by one of double the magnitude. Six or seven British machines would go off in formation and, taking their time, bomb Shumran scientifically. One bomb would be dropped on each run up wind over their hangars and sights corrected each time. Enemy anti-aircraft fire was inaccurate, and they never attempted to come up and engage. With all this practice the skill of the pilots increased, and the shooting became remarkably accurate. The enemy became dismayed; on the approach of British aeroplanes he would begin 'taxiing' his own round the aerodrome to make shooting more difficult. It was an interesting spectacle.

Paradoxically, a camaraderie grew up between British and German airmen here. The former even learnt the names of some of the enemy pilots. Schutz was considered a fine fighter, and a gentleman. Sometimes he would drop a note on the aerodrome asking them to send over the *Sketch* and the *Bystander* and stating that they were tired of the records captured with a gramophone at Kut, so would the British send them some new ones, especially *Tipperary*; in return for this the Germans would drop fresh vegetables from Baghdad. To the British, he seemed a sportsman and possessed a sense of humour. To prisoners he was known to be kind and courteous.

In Mesopotamia there were a few reserve machines at Amara and Basra, which could be flown up in perhaps a couple of days by pilots sent back from the front; outside of these the nearest source of supply was Egypt, three weeks away. There was no certainty of any relief owing to high demand elsewhere, and a fresh pilot from Britain might take anything up to eight or ten weeks to reach Mesopotamia. The Mediterranean route had been closed, so troops and material came half-way round the world, via the Cape, with perhaps long delays at Durban and Bombay. There was enough work in this theatre for three squadrons, but in December 1916, the Western Front was absorbing new units almost as fast as they were formed. No. 30 Squadron had to manage as best it could. As aircraft were so precious, all efforts had to be made to recover them. Tennant remembered,

In the evening a message came through that Lieuts. Chabot and Browning had been forced to land in front of our cavalry with a main strut shot away. For the benefit of the fresh air I flew out with a spare in order to get them back. The sun was setting as I arrived over the rearmost patrols, retiring by troops to their positions for the night; I could see Arab horsemen, showing up well in their flowing garments, hovering about on the flanks; I could also see the damaged aeroplane being dragged back by the cavalry. The ground was very broken, and it was necessary to land among the rear party, who were retiring steadily in open formation. As I came low one of the horses took fright, threw its 'sowar' [Indian cavalryman], and bolted, dragging the rider over the stony ground; he must have been killed. Events moved rapidly. It had been my intention to land, hand them the strut to take back to the machine, and clear off without stopping my engine. But the engine unfortunately stopped as I landed. A 'sowar' galloped up and took the strut while I endeavoured to start the engine single-handed. The last few 'sowars', thinking I was about to start, were retiring past me to the right and left, occasionally turning round to fire back at the 'Buddoos' (Arabs), who were blazing off their old 'bundooks' and spitting up the sand all round. It was rapidly growing dark, and the situation was unpleasant; in a moment I should be alone with these howling savages all round.

As I was exerting my best strength to start the propeller, a British officer fortunately came galloping back. Major

> Seeker, of the 14th Hussars; he had been an aerial observer in France. I leapt into my seat and he started me off, thereby saving an awkward situation. The damaged aeroplane was never recovered; the cavalry dragged it five miles, but to do so had to hack off its wings; the machine had to be left outside protection on account of a deep nullah filled with water; when the engine was regained it had been damaged beyond repair by Arabs.[18]

Finally, in August 1917, No. 63 Squadron arrived as reinforcements, and a number of R.E.8 aeroplanes had arrived in quantity for both squadrons; also the long-awaited Spad fighting scouts. There was no lack of support material, including rows of Crossley light lorries for desert transport. But every engine had to be taken down and overhauled; the aeroplane wooden parts had also shrunk in the heat, necessitating the rebuilding of many machines. The task of the Aeroplane Park was immense. Tennant flew the first Spad put together:

> … the cooling arrangements devised for Europe were inadequate, and the water started boiling as I left the ground. I shoved her up to try and get into cooler atmosphere. At 6,000 feet over the harbour I was suddenly aware of the whole top plane warping into wave-like contortions and steam scalding my face. The auxiliary water-tank in the plane had exploded and flooded the wood and fabric. It was very gingerly that I glided down, expecting the wings to carry away; my next breath was taken when the wheels touched the ground.[19]

Air operations in Macedonia bore some similarities to those in Mesopotamia. The terrain in northern Greece was equally inhospitable; mountainous and rugged, any forced landing away from the aerodrome was likely to end in death. Both sides employed machines that were generally slightly obsolete and were mainly used on photo reconnaissance missions. Unlike the situation on some of the other minor fronts, British airmen faced at times determined opposition in this theatre. The pre-eminent figure on the German side was Rudolf von Eschwege, known to the Bulgarians as 'the Eagle of the Aegean'. He operated from an airfield at Drama, and the German force consisted of three reconnaissance aircraft and a scout, covering a front of some 160km. Perhaps unusually, von Eschwege was an officer who took a keen interest in the technical aspects of his machines, even going so far as to work on his own engines. Hauptmann Heydemarck took over command of the Staffel immediately after his fourth victory. He remembered arriving at the aerodrome for the first time:

> Gradually the other officers made their appearance, the last of them being Lieutenant von Eschwege. He came from the aerodrome, where he had been at work on his engine. He was of medium height and almost delicate build. Two blue eyes shone from his sharply-cut face.
>
> 'I'm sorry I can't offer you my hand', he said with a smile, and held it out. It was as black as a locksmith's. His tunic and trousers were covered with oil smears. After he had retired to his room to wash, the others told me something about him. That was just like him, they said.

He loved his machine tenderly. Even in wet weather he spent the whole day on the aerodrome. After landing, it was seldom that he would allow his mechanics to attend to his machine unless he was with them. If his engine needed overhauling, he worked late into the night with his men. How often I saw him later sitting up by the engine in his overalls! When he returned after a brief interval, I congratulated him on his fourth victory.

'It was a pity the other Englishman bolted so quickly that I couldn't catch him up. It was a simpler job with my third. He seemed to be a greenhorn. He wasn't looking out, and so he let me come up unseen to within a hundred metres of him – and naturally that finished him.'

'Boelcke says, too, that the approach is the main thing.'

'He's right, he's right! If anyone asks me how I do it whether by flying or shooting – I say: 'Neither one nor the other! Just by approaching him!' Flying and shooting are part of the job; naturally, you've got to be all right in those matters. But the approach is the chief thing. On principle I only shoot when I'm within a hundred metres. And then the other machine has to fall'![20]

Lieutenants E.P. Hyde and Sydney Beare of No. 17 Squadron were Eschwege's fifth confirmed kill, the former officer remembering,

He was flying I believe a Halberstadt machine capable of doing 120 m.p.h. on the level and had the use of two guns synchronized with his propeller and he was a first

> class shot! Our Nieuport (new though it was) could achieve but 80 m.p.h. The odds were, of course, heavily against us and when Eschwege's bullets got through our gravity tank (not to mention our bodies) we had to land; what a very skilful landing Captain Beare made in spite of his injuries! We were, of course, in enemy territory. After a long delay we were taken to hospital at Boiran, thence later to Drama. Dr. Slavtcheff was the surgeon who attended to our wounds and he found it necessary to amputate my right foot. We shall always remember his kindness and sympathy to us in our sorry plight … Sidney Beare and I will always remember Eschwege's solicitude for us and our wounds. He brought to us in hospital gifts of chocolate, books and cigarettes.[21]

Eschwege had a reputation as a 'balloon-buster' and it was through this that he met his end. A booby-trapped balloon, with basket full of explosives and a dummy observer was raised; the German pilot took the bait, and when he dived in for the attack, the charge was detonated electrically from the ground. The explosion crippled his machine and he was killed. Overall, the air war in the sideshows was characterised by a far greater degree of improvisation than the campaign in Europe, which necessarily had first call on spares and equipment. To an even greater extent, local conditions also played a critical role in this, creating trying and difficult circumstances seldom found in Europe, and adding to the problem of shortages in both personnel and machinery.

Notes

Chapter One: 1914

1. James McCudden, *Five Years in the Royal Flying Corps*, London, 1918, p.29.
2. McCudden, p.33.
3. Walter Bloem, *The Advance From Mons*, London, 1930, p.36.
4. W. Read papers, Imperial War Museum, Department of Documents No. 13945.
5. *Liverpool Echo*, 3 September 1954.
6. Anon, *Hundert Briefe aus dem Felde; was die Soldaten über den Krieg Erzählen*, Nürnberg, 1915, p.85 (author's translation).
7. McCudden, p.41.
8. *I Was There*, Part 4, 1939.
9. *Barrovian*, March 1916, p.15.
10. McCudden, p.56.
11. *Aldershot News*, 23 April 1982.
12. *Reading Evening Post*, 13 April 1982.
13. *London Gazette*, 20 October 1914.
14. The National Archives, AIR 1/2301/212/7.
15. *Edinburgh Gazette*, 23 February 1915.
16. *Shrewsbury Chronicle*, 8 January 1915.
17. *Yorkshire Evening News*, 28 December 1914.

Chapter Two: Home Operations and Training

1. *British Medical Journal*, Vol. 287, 24–31 December 1983.
2. F.J. Adkin, *From the Ground Up* Shrewsbury, 1983, p.83.
3. Imperial War Museum, Sound Archive No. 3168 (author's transcript).
4. *Isle of Man Times*, 14 October 1916.

5. *Shields Daily News*, 2 June 1943.
6. Harold E. Hartney, *Up and at 'Em*, London, 1940, p.33.
7. http://www.worcestershireregiment.com/wr.php?main=inc/whs_chance_3.
8. Jon E. Lewis, *Mammoth Book of War Diaries & Letters*, London, 1998, p.337.
9. *Blackpool Gazette & Herald*, 8 June 1915.
10. *Coventry Evening Telegraph*, 28 July 1967.
11. *Stamford Mercury*, 7 October 1977.
12. *Farnborough News*, 31 March 1978.
13. *Stamford Mercury*, 31 March 1978.
14. Adkin, p.94.
15. *Reading Mercury*, 2 June 1917.
16. https://www.youtube.com/watch?v=qbOacwKsnrQ&t=78s (author's transcript).
17. Bert Frandsen, *Hat in the Ring: The Birth of American Air Power in the Great War*, Washington, 2010, p.124.

Chapter Three: Western Front, 1915–1916

1. Harold Rosher, *In the Royal Naval Air Service*, London, 1916, p.76.
2. The National Archives, AIR 2/165/MR10723.
3. Theo Osterkamp, *Du oder Ich*, Berlin, 1938, p.51.
4. *Leicester Daily Post*, 10 February 1916.
5. J.S. Castle papers, Liddle Collection, University of Leeds.
6. Hartney, p.54.
7. Hartney, p.61.
8. Hartney, p.66.
9. Georg Paul Neumann, *Die deutschen Luftstreitkräfte im Weltkriege*, Berlin, 1920, p.470.
10. Alfred J. Evans, *The Escaping Club*, London, 1921, p.3.
11. T. Stallibrass papers, Liddle Collection, University of Leeds.
12. Edward Packe, unpublished diary.
13. Cecil Lewis, Sir John Hammerton (editor), *The Great War ... I Was There!*, p.753.
14. Evans, p.5.

15. R.H.M.S. Saundby, *Flying Colours*, London, 1919.
16. Saundby.
17. Oswald Boelcke, (translated by Robert Reynold Hirsch), *An Aviator's Field Book,* New York, 1917, p.139.
18. Manfred von Richthofen, (translated by J. Ellis Barker), *The Red Battle Flyer*, New York, 1918, p.114.
19. Max Zeidelhack, *Bayerische Flieger im Weltkrieg; Ein Buch der Taten und Erinnerungen*, Munich, 1919, p.80.
20. The National Archives, AIR1/2388/228/11/84.
21. The National Archives, AIR 76/255/56.
22. Alan Bott, *An Airman's Outings*, London, 1917, p.41.
23. Bott, p.42.
24. Boelcke, p.192.
25. Frank T. Courtney, *Flight Path: My Fifty Years of Aviation*, London, 1972, p.95.
26. Gerald Featherstone Knight, *Brother Bosch: An Airman's Escape from Germany*, London, 1919, p.5.
27. C.P.O. Bartlett, *Aeroplane Monthly*, August 1974.
28. Bartlett, *op cit.*

Chapter Four: Western Front, 1917–1918

1. Barlett, *op cit.*
2. E.D. Crundall, *Fighter Pilot on the Western Front*, London, 1975, p.50.
3. *Thomson's Weekly News*, 19 May 1917.
4. *Oban Times and Argyllshire Advertiser*, 19 May 1917.
5. Harold Balfour papers, Liddle Collection, University of Leeds.
6. The National Archives, WO339/54312.
7. Spin, *Short Flights With the Cloud Cavalry*, London, 1918, p.63.
8. *London Gazette*, 18 June 1917.
9. *London Gazette*, 3 December 1918.
10. RAF museum archive.
11. Adkin, p.58.
12. Manx Aviation Preservation Society archive, MAPS367.
13. W.G. McMinnies, *Practical Flying,* London, 1918, p.212.

14. The National Archives, MH106/2202-2206.
15. The National Archives, AIR1/2390/228/11/219.
16. The National Archives, AIR1/2390/228/11/119.
17. Ernst Udet, *Ace of the Black Cross*, London, 2013, p.31.
18. Udet, p.82.
19. Walter Noble, *With A Bristol Fighter Squadron*, London, 1920, p.51.
20. *Cross and Cockade (USA)*, Vol. 10, No. 1, 1969, pp.34–54.
21. *Belfast Telegraph*, 29 March 1968.
22. *Belfast Telegraph*, 30 March 1968.
23. *Isle of Man Examiner*, 16 May 1989.
24. *op cit.*
25. *op cit.*
26. *op cit.*
27. Imperial War Museum, Sound Archive No. 12099 (author's transcript).
28. Jack Warner, *Jack of All Trades*, London, 1975, p.25.
29. Warner, p.26.
30. Courtney, p.116.
31. *Cross & Cockade (Great Britain)*, Vol. 9, No. 3.
32. *Cross & Cockade International Journal*, Vol. 40, No. 2.
33. *Isle of Man Examiner*, 16 May 1989.
34. Robert H. Reece, *Night Bombing With the Bedouins* Boston, Massachutsetts, 1919, p.44.
35. *Coventry Evening Telegraph*, 3 January 1986.
36. *Harrow Midweek*, 17 February 1981.
37. *op cit.*
38. *Bury Free Press*, 20 November 1970.

Chapter Five: Mediterranean, Aegean and the Persian Gulf

1. Geoffrey Bromet diary, Liddle Collection, University of Leeds.
2. *op cit.*
3. Air Commodore Sampson papers, Imperial War Museum, Department of Documents.
4. Stephen Roskill, *The Royal Naval Air Service*, London, 1969, p.222.

5. *Maidenhead Advertiser*, 23 June 1915.
6. Richard Bell Davies, *Sailor in the Air*, London, 1967, p.127.
7. Charles Rumney Samson, *Fights and Flights*, London, 1930, p.229.
8. *London Gazette*, 14 January 1916.
9. Bromet, *op cit.*
10. Bell Davies, p.127.
11. Peter Liddle, *Men of Gallipoli*, London, 1976, p.235.
12. William Wedgwood Benn, *In the Sideshows*, London, 1919, p.78.
13. Wedgwood Benn, p.147.
14. *Eckington, Woodhouse and Staveley Express*, 2 December 1916.
15. *Eckington, Woodhouse and Staveley Express*, 30 December 1916.
16. *Edinburgh Gazette*, 17 November 1916.
17. John Edward Tennant, *In the Clouds Above Baghdad*, London, 1920, p.21.
18. Tennant, p.61.
19. Tennant, p.194.
20. Georg Wilhelm Heydemarck, *War Flying in Macedonia*, London, 1935, p.22.
21. Heydermarck, p.7.

Bibliography

Anonymous, *Hundert Briefe aus dem Felde; was die Soldaten über den Krieg Erzählen*, Nürnberg, 1915.

Adkin, Fred, *From the Ground Up*, Shrewsbury, 1983.

Barker, Stephen, *The Flying Sikh*, Barnsley, 2022.

Bell Davies, Richard, *Sailor in the Air*, London, 1967.

Bewsher, Paul, *Green Balls*, London, 1919.

Bishop, William Avery, *Winged Warfare*, London, 1918.

Blake, Wilfrid Theodore, *Plane Tales From the Skies*, London, 1918.

Bloem, Walter, *The Advance from Mons*, London, 1930.

Bott, Alan, *An Airman's Outings*, London, 1917.

Burns, Ian M., *Ben-My-Chree Woman of My Heart: Isle of Man Packet Steamer and Seaplane Carrier*, Leicester, 2008.

Courtney, Frank T., *Flight Path*, London, 1972.

Crundall, E.D., *Fighter Pilot on the Western Front*, London, 1975.

Douglas, Sholto, *Years of Combat*, London, 1963.

Evans, Alfred John, *The Escaping Club*, London, 1921.

Frandsen, Bert *Hat in the Ring: The Birth of American Air Power in the Great War*, Washington, 2010.

Gurdon, John Everard, *The German Air Force in the Great War*, London, 1921.

Hartney, Harold E., *Up and At 'Em*, London, 1940.

Heydemarck, Georg Wilhelm (translated by Claude W. Sykes), *War Flying in Macedonia*, London, 1935.

Hodges, Goderick, *Memoires of an Old Balloonatic*, London, 1977.

Jefford, C.G., *Observers and Navigators and Other Non-Pilot Aircrew in the RFC, RNAS and RAF*, London, 2014.

Knight, Gerald Featherstone, *Brother Bosch: An Airman's Escape from Germany*, London, 1919.

Lea, John, *Reggie: The Life of Air Vice Marshal R.L.G. Marix*, Edinburgh, 1994.

Lee, A.S.G., *No Parachute*, New York, 1970.
Lewis, Cecil, *Sagittarius Rising*, London, 1936.
Lewis, Gwilym Hugh, *Wings over the Somme, 1916–1918*, London, 1976.
Liddle Peter H., *Men of Gallipoli*, London, 1976.
Liddle, Peter H., *The Airman's War*, Blandford, 1987.
Liddle, Peter H., *Captured Memories 1900–1918*, Barnsley, 2011.
Long, Selden Herbert, *In The Blue*, London, 1920.
McCudden, James, *Five Years in the Royal Flying Corps*, London, 1918.
MacLanachan, W., *Fighter Pilot*, London, 1936.
MacMillan, Norman, *Offensive Patrol the Story of the RNAS, RFC and RAF in Italy, 1917–18*, London, 1973.
McMinnies, W.G., *Practical Flying*, London, 1918.
Middleton, Edgar Charles, *The Way of the Air*, London, 1917.
Middleton, Edgar Charles, *Tails Up*, London, 1918.
Noble, Walter, *With A Bristol Fighter Squadron*, London, 1920.
Osterkamp, Theo, *Du oder Ich*, Berlin, 1938.
Poolman, Kenneth, *Zeppelins over England*, London, 1960.
Reece, Robert H., *Night Bombing With the Bedouins*, Boston, Massachutsetts, 1919.
Roberts, E.M., *A Flying Fighter*, New York, 1918.
Rosher, Harold, *In the Royal Naval Air Service*, London, 1916.
Roskill, Stephen, *The Royal Naval Air Service*, London, 1969.
Samson, Charles Rumney, *Fights and Flights*, London, 1930.
Saundby, R.H.M.S., *Flying Colours*, London, 1919.
Saunders, Hilary St George, *Per Ardua: The Rise of British Air Power*, London, 1944.
'Spin' (pseudonym G.E. Thomson), *Short Flights With the Cloud Cavalry*, London, 1918.
Strange, L.A., *Recollections of an Airman*, London, 1933.
Tennant, John Edward, *In the Clouds Above Baghdad*, London, 1920.
Udet, Ernst, *Ace of the Black Cross*, London, 1937.
Warner, Jack, *Jack of All Trades*, London, 1975.
Wedgwood Benn, William, *In the Side Shows*, London, 1919.
'Wing Adjutant', *The Royal Flying Corps in the War*, New York, 1918.

Index